The Vision of Hamilton

Alexander Hamilton and Lyndon LaRouche

The Vision of Hamilton:
Four Writings by Alexander Hamilton and
The "Four Laws" of Lyndon LaRouche

Edited by Jason Ross

EIR News Service, Inc. • Washington, D.C.

Layout: Jason Ross
Source material: Michael Carr
Cover design: Matthew Ogden
Cover photo: Alan Scott Walker

PREFACE

This republication of Hamilton's four great economic works comes at the instigation of American economist Lyndon LaRouche, who has stressed the urgency for an understanding of Hamilton's economic outlook to confront the profound economic crisis now erupting within the trans-Atlantic financial system.

Hamilton's vision for the newly created United States was of an industrializing nation in which the human ability to develop and grow would lead to new technologies, new resources, and a national commitment to the future. This outlook, and the lessons to be learned from Hamilton's success, are of timely importance today.

These four writings comprise three reports to the Congress—his Report on Public Credit, Report on a National Bank, and Report on Manufactures—and his Opinion as to the Constitutionality of the Bank of the United States. Together, these documents represent the kernel of Hamilton's thought, and the basis upon which the United States grew from a small agricultural nation to the world's leading economy.

Applying this outlook to the present, we include, following Hamilton's writings, Lyndon LaRouche's 2014 policy proposal for "Four New Laws to Save the U.S.A. Now."

This is a handbook for needed economic growth today.

CONTENTS

Alexander Hamilton, by John Trumbull

Report on Public Credit

January 1790

To the Speaker of the House of Representatives:

The Secretary of the Treasury, in obedience to the resolution of the House of Representatives, of the twenty-first day of September last, has, during the recess of Congress, applied himself to the consideration of a proper plan for the support of the Public Credit, with all the attention which was due to the authority of the House, and to the magnitude of the object.

In the discharge of this duty, he has felt, in no small degree, the anxieties which naturally flow from a just estimate of the difficulty of the task, from a well-founded diffidence of his own qualifications for executing it with success, and from a deep and solemn conviction of the momentous nature of the truth contained in the resolution under which his investigations have been conducted, "That an adequate provision for the support of the Public Credit, is a matter of high importance to the honor and prosperity of the United States."

With an ardent desire that his well-meant endeavors may be conducive to the real advantage of the nation, and with the utmost deference to the superior judgment of the House, he now respectfully submits the result of his enquiries and reflections, to their indulgent construction.

In the opinion of the Secretary, the wisdom of the House, in giving their explicit sanction to the proposition which has been stated, cannot but be applauded by all, who will seriously consider, and trace through their obvious consequences, these plain and undeniable truths.

That exigencies are to be expected to occur, in the affairs of nations, in which there will be a necessity for borrowing.

That loans in times of public danger, especially from foreign war, are found an indispensable resource, even to the wealthiest of them.

And that in a country, which, like this, is possessed of little active wealth, or in other words, little monied capital, the necessity for that resource, must, in such emergencies, be proportionably urgent.

And as on the one hand, the necessity for borrowing in particular emergencies cannot be doubted, so on the other, it is equally evident, that to be able to borrow upon *good terms*, it is essential that the credit of a nation should be well established.

For when the credit of a country is in any degree questionable, it never fails to give an extravagant premium, in one shape or another, upon all the loans it has occasion to make. Nor does the evil end here; the same disadvantage must be sustained upon whatever is to be bought on terms of future payment.

From this constant necessity of *borrowing* and *buying dear*, it is easy to conceive how immensely the expenses of a nation, in a course of time, will be augmented by an unsound state of the public credit.

To attempt to enumerate the complicated variety of mischiefs in the whole system of the social economy, which proceed from a neglect of the maxims that uphold public credit, and justify the solicitude manifested by the House on this point, would be an improper intrusion on their time and patience.

In so strong a light nevertheless do they appear to the Secretary, that on their due observance at the present critical juncture, materially depends, in his judgment, the individual and aggregate prosperity of the citizens of the United States; their relief from the embarrassments they now experience; their character as a People; the cause of good government.

If the maintenance of public credit, then, be truly so important, the next enquiry which suggests itself is, by what means it is to be effected? The ready answer to which question is, by good faith, by a punctual performance of contracts. States, like individuals, who observe their engagements, are respected and trusted: while the reverse is the fate of those, who pursue an opposite conduct.

Every breach of the public engagements, whether from choice or necessity, is in different degrees hurtful to public credit. When such a necessity does truly exist, the evils of it are only to be palliated by a scrupulous attention, on the part of the government, to carry the violation no farther than the necessity absolutely requires, and to manifest, if the nature of the case admits of it, a sincere disposition to make reparation, whenever circumstances shall permit. But with every possible mitigation, credit must suffer, and numerous mischiefs ensue. It is therefore highly important, when an appearance of necessity seems to press upon the public councils, that they should examine well its reality, and be perfectly assured, that there is no method of escaping from it, before they yield to its suggestions. For though it cannot safely be affirmed, that occasions have never existed, or may not exist, in which violations of the public faith, in this respect, are inevitable; yet there is great reason to believe, that they exist far less frequently than precedents indicate; and are oftenest either pretended through levity, or want of firmness, or supposed through want of knowledge. Expedients might often have been devised to effect, consistently with good faith, what has been done in contravention of it. Those who are most commonly creditors of a nation, are, generally speaking, enlightened men; and there are signal examples to warrant a conclusion, that when a candid and fair appeal is made to them, they will understand their true interest too well to refuse their concurrence in such modifications of their claims, as any real necessity may demand.

While the observance of that good faith, which is the basis of public credit, is recommended by the strongest inducements of political expediency, it is enforced by considerations of still greater authority. There are arguments for it, which rest on the immutable principles of moral obligation. And in proportion as the mind is disposed to contemplate, in the order of Providence, an intimate connection between public virtue and public happiness, will be its repugnancy to a violation of those principles.

This reflection derives additional strength from the nature of the debt of the United States. It was the price of liberty. The faith of America has been repeatedly pledged for it, and with solemnities, that give peculiar force to the obligation. There is indeed reason to regret that it has not hitherto been kept; that the necessities of the war, conspiring with inexperience in the subjects of finance, produced direct infractions; and that the subsequent period has been a continued scene of negative violation, or non-compliance. But a diminution of this regret arises from the reflection, that the last seven years have exhibited an earnest and uniform effort, on the part of the government of the union, to retrieve the national credit, by doing justice to the creditors of the nation; and that the embarrassments of a defective constitution, which defeated this laudable effort, have ceased.

From this evidence of a favorable disposition, given by the former government, the institution of a new one, clothed with powers competent to calling forth the resources of the community, has excited correspondent expectations. A general belief, accordingly, prevails, that the credit of the United States will quickly be established on the firm foundation of an effectual provision for the existing debt. The influence, which this has had at home, is witnessed by the rapid increase, that has taken place in the market value of the public securities. From January to November, they rose thirty-three and a third percent, and from that period to this time, they have risen fifty percent more. And the intelligence from abroad announces effects proportionably favorable to our national credit and consequence.

It cannot but merit particular attention, that among ourselves the most enlightened friends of good government are those, whose expectations are the highest.

To justify and preserve their confidence; to promote the

increasing respectability of the American name; to answer the calls of justice; to restore landed property to its due value; to furnish new resources both to agriculture and commerce; to cement more closely the union of the states; to add to their security against foreign attack; to establish public order on the basis of an upright and liberal policy. These are the great and invaluable ends to be secured, by a proper and adequate provision, at the present period, for the support of public credit.

To this provision we are invited, not only by the general considerations, which have been noticed, but by others of a more particular nature. It will procure to every class of the community some important advantages, and remove some no less important disadvantages.

The advantage to the public creditors from the increased value of that part of their property which constitutes the public debt, needs no explanation.

But there is a consequence of this, less obvious, though not less true, in which every other citizen is interested. It is a well known fact, that in countries in which the national debt is properly funded, and an object of established confidence, it answers most of the purposes of money. Transfers of stock or public debt are there equivalent to payments in specie; or in other words, stock, in the principal transactions of business, passes current as specie. The same thing would, in all probability happen, here, under the like circumstances.

The benefits of this are various and obvious.

First. Trade is extended by it; because there is a larger capital to carry it on, and the merchant can at the same time, afford to trade for smaller profits; as his stock, which, when unemployed, brings him in an interest from the government, serves him also as money, when he has a call for it in his commercial operations.

Secondly. Agriculture and manufactures are also promoted by it: For the like reason, that more capital can be commanded to be employed in both; and because the merchant, whose enterprise in foreign trade, gives to them activity and extension, has greater means for enterprise.

Thirdly. The interest of money will be lowered by it; for this is always in a ratio, to the quantity of money, and to the quickness of circulation. This circumstance will enable both the public and individuals to borrow on easier and cheaper terms.

And from the combination of these effects, additional aids will be furnished to labor, to industry, and to arts of every kind.

But these good effects of a public debt are only to be looked for, when, by being well funded, it has acquired an *adequate* and *stable* value. Till then, it has rather a contrary tendency. The fluctuation and insecurity incident to it in an unfunded state, render it a mere commodity, and a precarious one. As such, being only an object of occasional and particular speculation, all the money applied to it is so much diverted from the more useful channels of circulation, for which the thing itself affords no substitute: So that, in fact, one serious inconvenience of an unfunded debt is, that it contributes to the scarcity of money.

This distinction which has been little if at all attended to, is of the greatest moment. It involves a question immediately interesting to every part of the community; which is no other than this—Whether the public debt, by a provision for it on true principles, shall be rendered a *substitute* for money; or whether, by being left as it is, or by being provided for in such a manner as will wound those principles, and destroy confidence, it shall be suffered to continue, as it is, a pernicious drain of our cash from the channels of productive industry.

The effect, which the funding of the public debt, on right principles, would have upon landed property, is one of the circumstances attending such an arrangement, which has been least adverted to, though it deserves the most particular attention.

The present depreciated state of that species of property is a serious calamity. The value of cultivated lands, in most of the states, has fallen since the revolution from 25 to 50 percent. In those farthest south, the decrease is still more considerable. Indeed, if the representations, continually received from that quarter, may be credited, lands there will command no price, which may not be deemed an almost total sacrifice.

This decrease, in the value of lands, ought, in a great measure, to be attributed to the scarcity of money. Consequently whatever produces an augmentation of the monied capital of the country, must have a proportional effect in raising that value. The beneficial tendency of a funded debt, in this respect, has been manifested by the most decisive experience in Great-Britain.

The proprietors of lands would not only feel the benefit of this increase in the value of their property, and of a more prompt and better sale, when they had occasion to sell; but the necessity of selling would be, itself, greatly diminished. As the same cause would contribute to the facility of loans, there is reason to believe, that such of them as are indebted, would be able through that resource, to satisfy their more urgent creditors.

It ought not however to be expected, that the advantages, described as likely to result from funding the public debt, would be instantaneous. It might require some time to bring the value of stock to its natural level, and to attach to it that fixed confidence, which is necessary to its quality as money. Yet the late rapid rise of the public securities encourages an expectation, that the progress of stock to the desirable point, will be much more expeditious than could have been foreseen. And as in the mean time it will be increasing in value, there is room to conclude, that it will, from the outset, answer many of the purposes in contemplation. Particularly it seems to be probable, that from creditors, who are not themselves necessitous, it will early meet with a ready reception in payment of debts, at its current price.

Having now taken a concise view of the inducements to a proper provision for the public debt, the next enquiry which presents itself is, what ought to be the nature of such a provision? This requires some preliminary discussions.

It is agreed on all hands, that that part of the debt which has been contracted abroad, and is denominated the foreign debt, ought to be provided for, according to the precise terms of the contracts relating to it. The discussions, which can arise, therefore, will have reference essentially to the domestic part of it, or to that which has been contracted at home. It is to be regretted, that there is not the same unanimity of sentiment on this part, as on the other.

The Secretary has too much deference for the opinions of every part of the community, not to have observed one, which has, more than once, made its appearance in the public prints, and which is occasionally to be met with in conversation. It involves this question, whether a discrimination ought not to be made between original holders of the public securities, and present possessors, by purchase. Those who advocate a discrimination are for making a full provision for the securities of the former, at their nominal value; but contend, that the latter ought to receive no more than the cost to them, and the interest: And the idea is sometimes suggested of making good the difference to the primitive possessor.

In favor of this scheme, it is alleged, that it would be unreasonable to pay twenty shillings in the pound, to one who had not given more for it than three or four. And it is added, that it would be hard to aggravate the misfortune of the first owner, who, probably through necessity, parted with his property at so great a loss, by obliging him to contribute to the profit of the person, who had speculated on his distresses.

The Secretary, after the most mature reflection on the force of this argument, is induced to reject the doctrine it contains, as equally unjust and impolitic, as highly injurious, even to the original holders of public securities; as ruinous to public credit.

It is inconsistent with justice, because in the first place, it is a breach of contract; in violation of the rights of a fair purchaser.

The nature of the contract in its origin, is, that the public will pay the sum expressed in the security, to the first holder, or his *assignee*. The *intent*, in making the security assignable, is, that the proprietor may be able to make use of his property, by selling it for as much as it *may be worth in the market*, and that the buyer may be *safe* in the purchase.

Every buyer therefore stands exactly in the place of the seller, has the same right with him to the identical sum expressed in the security, and having acquired that right, by fair purchase, and in conformity to the original *agreement* and *intention* of the government, his claim cannot be disputed, without manifest injustice.

That he is to be considered as a fair purchaser, results from this: Whatever necessity the seller may have been under, was occasioned by the government, in not making a proper provision for its debts. The buyer had no agency in it, and therefore ought not to suffer. He is not even chargeable with having taken an undue advantage. He paid what the commodity was worth in the market, and took the risks of reimbursement upon himself. He of course gave a fair equivalent, and ought to reap the benefit of his hazard; a hazard which was far from inconsiderable, and which, perhaps, turned on little less than a revolution in government.

That the case of those, who parted with their securities from necessity, is a hard one, cannot be denied. But whatever complaint of injury, or claim of redress, they may have, respects the government solely. They have not only nothing to object to the persons who relieved their necessities, by giving them the current price of their property, but they are even under an implied condition to contribute to the reimbursement of those persons. They knew, that by the terms of the contract with themselves, the public were bound to pay to those, to whom they should convey their title, the sums stipulated to be paid to them; and, as citizens of the United States, they were to bear their proportion of the contribution for that purpose. This, by the act of assignment, they tacitly engage to do; and if they had an option, they could not, with integrity or good faith, refuse to do it, without the consent of those to whom they sold.

But though many of the original holders sold from necessity, it does not follow, that this was the case with all of them. It may well be supposed, that some of them did it either through want of confidence in an eventual provision, or from the allurements of some profitable speculation. How shall these different classes be discriminated from each other? How shall it be ascertained, in any case, that the money, which the original holder obtained for his security, was not more beneficial to him, than if he had held it to the present time, to avail himself of the provision which shall be made? How shall it be known, whether if the purchaser had employed his money in some other way, he would not be in a better situation, than by having applied it in the purchase of securities, though he should now receive their full amount? And if neither of these things can be known, how shall it be determined whether a discrimination, independent of the breach of contract, would not do a real injury to purchasers; and if it included a compensation to the primitive proprietors, would not give them an advantage, to which they had no equitable pretension.

It may well be imagined, also, that there are not wanting instances, in which individuals, urged by a present necessity, parted with the securities received by them from the public, and shortly after replaced them with others, as an indemnity for their first loss. Shall they be deprived of the indemnity which they have endeavoured to secure by so provident an arrangement?

Questions of this sort, on a close inspection, multiply themselves without end, and demonstrate the injustice of a discrimination, even on the most subtile calculations of equity, abstracted from the obligation of contract.

The difficulties too of regulating the details of a plan for that purpose, which would have even the semblance of equity, would be found immense. It may well be doubted whether they would not be insurmountable, and replete with such absurd, as well as inequitable consequences, as to disgust even the proposers of the measure.

As a specimen of its capricious operation, it will be sufficient to notice the effect it would have upon two persons, who may be supposed two years ago to have purchased, each, securities at three shillings in the pound, and one of them to retain those bought by him, till the discrimination should take place; the other to have parted with those bought by him, within a month past, in nine shillings. The former, who had had most confidence in the government, would in this case only receive at the rate of three shillings and the interest; while the latter, who had had less confidence would receive for *what cost him the same money* at the rate of nine shillings, and his representative, *standing in his place*, would be entitled to a like rate.

The impolicy of a discrimination results from two considerations; one, that it proceeds upon a principle destructive of that *quality* of the public debt, or the stock of the nation, which is essential to its capacity for answering the purposes of money—that is the *security* of *transfer*; the other, that as well on this account, as because it includes a breach of faith, it renders property in the funds less valuable; consequently induces lenders to demand a higher premium for what they lend, and produces every other inconvenience of a bad state of public credit.

It will be perceived at first sight, that the transferable quality of stock is essential to its operation as money, and that this depends on the idea of complete security to the transferee, and a firm persuasion, that no distinction can in any circumstances be made between him and the original proprietor.

The precedent of an invasion of this fundamental principle, would of course tend to deprive the community of an advantage, with which no temporary saving could bear the least comparison.

And it will as readily be perceived, that the same cause would operate a diminution of the value of stock in the hands of the first, as well as of every other holder. The price, which any man, who should incline to purchase, would be willing to give for it, would be in a compound ratio to the immediate profit it afforded, and to the chance of the continuance of his profit. If there was supposed to be any hazard of the latter, the risk would be taken into the calculation, and either there would be no purchase at all, or it would be at a proportionably less price.

For this diminution of the value of stock, every person, who should be about to lend to the government, would demand a compensation; and would add to the actual difference, between the nominal and the market value, and equivalent for the chance of greater decrease; which, in a precarious state of public credit, is always to be taken into the account.

Every compensation of this sort, it is evident, would be an absolute loss to the government.

In the preceding discussion of the impolicy of a discrimination, the injurious tendency of it to those, who continue to be the holders of the securities, they received from the government, has been explained. Nothing need be added, on this head, except that this is an additional and interesting light, in which the injustice of the measure may be seen. It would not only divest present proprietors by purchase, of the rights they had acquired under the sanction of public faith, but it would depreciate the property of the remaining original holders.

It is equally unnecessary to add any thing to what has been already said to demonstrate the fatal influence, which the principle of discrimination would have on the public credit.

But there is still a point in view in which it will appear perhaps even more exceptionable, than in either of the former. It would be repugnant to an express provision of the Constitution of the United States. This provision is, that "all debts contracted and engagements entered into before the adoption of that Constitution shall be as valid against the United States under it, as under the confederation," which amounts to a constitutional ratification of the contracts respecting the debt, in the state in which they existed under the confederation. And resorting to that standard, there can be no doubt, that the rights of assignees and original holders, must be considered as equal.

In exploding thus fully the principle of discrimination, the Secretary is happy in reflecting, that he is the only advocate of what has been already sanctioned by the formal and express authority of the government of the Union, in these emphatic terms—"The remaining class of creditors (say Congress in their circular address to the states, of the 26th of April 1783) is composed, partly of such of our fellow-citizens as originally lent to the public the use of their funds, or have since manifested *most confidence* in their country, by receiving transfers from the lenders; and partly of those, whose property has been either advanced or assumed for the public service. To *discriminate* the merits of these several descriptions of creditors, would be a task equally unnecessary and invidious. If the voice of humanity plead more loudly in favor of some than of others, the voice of policy, no less than of justice, pleads in favor of all. A WISE NATION will never permit those who relieve the wants of their country, or who *rely most* on its *faith*, its *firmness*, and its *resources*, when either of them is distrusted, to suffer by the event."

The Secretary concluding, that a discrimination, between the different classes of creditors of the United States, cannot with propriety be *made*, proceeds to examine whether a difference ought to be permitted to *remain* between them, and another description of public creditors—Those of the states individually.

The Secretary, after mature reflection on this point, entertains a full conviction, that an assumption of the debts of the particular states by the union, and a like provision for them, as for those of the union, will be a measure of sound policy and substantial justice.

It would, in the opinion of the Secretary, contribute, in an eminent degree, to an orderly, stable and satisfactory arrangement of the national finances.

Admitting, as ought to be the case, that a provision must be made, in some way or other, for the entire debt, it will follow that no greater revenues will be required whether that provision be made wholly by the United States, or partly by them and partly by the states separately.

The principal question, then, must be whether such a provision cannot be more conveniently and effectually made by one general plan, issuing from one authority, than by different plans, originating in different authorities?

In the first case there can be no competition for resources; in the last there must be such a competition. The consequences of this, without the greatest caution on both sides, might be interfering regulations, and thence collision and confusion. Particular branches of industry might also be oppressed by it. The most productive objects of revenue are not numerous. Either these must be wholly engrossed by one side, which might lessen the efficacy of the provisions by the other, or both must have recourse to the same objects, in different modes, which might occasion an accumulation upon them beyond what they could properly bear. If this should not happen, the caution requisite to avoiding it would prevent the revenue's deriving the full benefit of each object. The danger of interference and of excess would be apt to impose restraints very unfriendly to the complete command of those resources which are the most convenient, and to compel the having recourse to others, less eligible in themselves and less agreeable to the community.

The difficulty of an effectual command of the public resources, in case of separate provisions for the debt, may be seen in another, and, perhaps, more striking light. It would naturally happen that different states, from local considerations, would, in some instances, have recourse to different objects, in others to the same objects, in different degrees, for procuring the funds of which they stood in need. It is easy to conceive how this diversity would affect the aggregate revenue of the country. By the supposition, articles which yielded a full supply in some states would yield nothing, or an insufficient product, in others. And hence, the public revenue would not derive the full benefit of those articles from state regulations; neither could the deficiencies be made good by those of the Union. It is a provision of the national Constitution that "all duties, imposts, and excises shall be uniform throughout the United States." And, as the General Government would be under a necessity, from motives of policy, of paying regard to the duty which may have been previously imposed upon any article, though but in a single state, it would be constrained either to refrain wholly from any further imposition upon such article, where it had been already rated as high as was proper, or to confine itself to the difference between the existing rate and what the article would reasonably bear. Thus the pre-occupancy of an article by a single state would tend to arrest or abridge the impositions of the Union on that article. And as it is supposable that a great variety of articles might be placed in this situation, by dissimilar arrangements of the particular states, it is evident that the aggregate revenue of the country would be likely to be very materially contracted by the plan of separate provisions.

If all the public creditors receive their dues from one source, distributed with an equal hand, their interest will be the same. And, having the same interests, they will unite in the support of the fiscal arrangements of the Government—as these, too, can be made with more convenience where there is no competition. These circumstances combined will insure to the revenue laws a more ready and more satisfactory execution.

If, on the contrary, there are distinct provisions, there will be distinct interests, drawing different ways. That union and concert of views among the creditors, which in every Government is of great importance to their security and to that of public credit, will not only not exist, but will be likely to give place to mutual jealousy and opposition. And from this cause the operation of the systems which may be adopted, both by the particular states and by the Union, with relation to their respective debts, will be in danger of being counteracted.

There are several reasons which render it probable that the situation of the state creditors would be worse than that of the creditors of the Union, if there be not a national assumption of the state debts. Of these it will be sufficient to mention two: one, that a principal branch of revenue is exclusively vested in the Union; the other, that a state must always be checked in the imposition of taxes on articles of consumption, from the want of power to extend the same regulation to the other states, and from the tendency of partial duties to injure its industry and commerce. Should the state creditors stand upon a less eligible footing than the others, it is unnatural to expect they would see with pleasure a provision for them. The influence which their dissatisfaction might have, could not but operate injuriously, both for the creditors and the credit of the United States.

Hence it is even the interest of the creditors of the Union, that those of the individual states should be comprehended in a general provision. Any attempt to secure to the former either exclusive or peculiar advantages, would materially hazard their interests.

Neither would it be just that one class of public creditors should be more favored than the other. The objects for which both descriptions of the debt were contracted are in the main the same. Indeed, a great part of the particular debts of the states has arisen from assumptions by them on account of the Union. And it is most equitable that there should be the same measure of retribution for all.

There is an objection, however, to an assumption of the state debts, which deserves particular notice.

It may be supposed that it would increase the difficulty of an equitable settlement between them and the United States.

The principles of that settlement, whenever they shall be discussed, will require all the moderation and wisdom of the Government. In the opinion of the Secretary, that discussion, till further lights are obtained, would be premature.

All, therefore, which he would now think advisable on the point in question would be that the amount of the debts assumed and provided for should be charged to the respective states to abide an eventual arrangement. This the United States, as assignees to the creditors, would have an indisputable right to do.

But, as it might be a satisfaction to the House to have before them some plan for the liquidation of accounts between the Union and its members, which, including the assumption of the state debts, would consist with equity, the Secretary will submit, in this place, such thoughts on the subject as have occurred to his own mind, or been suggested to him, most compatible, in his judgment, with the end proposed.

Let each state be charged with all the money advanced to it out of the treasury of the United States, liquidated according to the specie value at the time of each advance, with interest at six percent.

Let it also be charged with the amount, in specie value, of all its securities which shall be assumed, with the interest upon them, to the time when interest shall become payable by the United States.

Let it be credited for all moneys paid and articles furnished to the United States, and for all other expenditures during the war, either toward general or particular defence, whether authorized or unauthorized by the United States; the whole liquidated to specie value, and bearing an interest of six percent from the several times at which the several payments, advances, and expenditures accrued.

And let all sums of continental money, now in the treasuries of the respective states, which shall be paid into the treasury of the United States, be credited at specie value.

Upon a statement of the accounts according to these principles, there can be little doubt that balances would appear in favor of all the states against the United States.

To equalize the contributions of the states, let each be then charged with its proportion of the aggregate of those balances, according to some equitable ratio, to be devised for that purpose.

If the contributions should be found disproportionate, the result of this adjustment would be, that some states would be creditors, some debtors, to the Union.

Should this be the case—as it will be attended with less inconvenience to the United States to have to pay balances to, than to receive them from, the particular States—it may, perhaps, be practicable to effect the former by a second process, in the nature of a transfer of the amount of the debts of debtor states, to the credit of creditor states, observing the ratio by which the first apportionment shall have been made. This, whilst it would destroy the balances due from the former, would increase those due to the latter; these to be provided for by the United States, at a reasonable interest, but not to be transferable.

The expediency of this second process must depend on a knowledge of the result of the first. If the inequalities should be too great, the arrangement may be impracticable, without unduly increasing the debt of the United States. But it is not likely that this would be the case. It is also to be remarked, that though this second process might not, upon the principle of apportionment, bring the thing to the point aimed at, yet it may approach so nearly to it, as to avoid essentially the embarrassment of having considerable balances to collect from any of the states.

The whole of this arrangement to be under the superintendence of commissioners, vested with equitable discretion and final authority. The operation of the plan is exemplified in Schedule A.

The general principle of it seems to be equitable: for it appears difficult to conceive a good reason why the expenses for the particular defence of a part, in a common war, should not be a common charge, as well as those incurred professedly for the general defence. The defence of each part is that of the whole; and unless all the expenditures are brought into a common mass, the tendency must be to add to the calamities suffered, by being the most exposed to the ravages of war, an increase of burdens.

This plan seems to be susceptible of no objection which does not belong to every other, that proceeds on the idea of a final adjustment of accounts. The difficulty of settling a ratio is common to all. This must, probably, either be sought for in the proportions of the requisitions during the war, or in the decision of commissioners, appointed with plenary power. The rule prescribed in the Constitution, with regard to representation and direct taxes, would evidently not be applicable to the situation of parties during the period in question.

The existing debt of the United States is excluded from the computation, as it ought to be, because it will be provided for out of a general fund.

The only discussion of a preliminary kind which remains, relates to the distinctions of the debt into principal and interest. It is well known that the arrears of the latter bear a large proportion to the amount of the former. The immediate payment of these arrears is evidently impracticable; and a question arises, What ought to be done with them?

There is good reason to conclude, that the impressions of many are more favorable to the claim of the principal, than to that of the interest; at least so far as to produce an opinion, that an inferior provision might suffice for the latter.

But, to the Secretary, this opinion does not appear to be well founded. His investigations of the subject have led him to a conclusion, that the arrears of interest have pretensions at least equal to the principal.

The liquidated debt, traced to its origin, falls under two principal discriminations. One relating to loans, the other to services performed and articles supplied.

The part arising from loans was at first made payable at fixed periods, which have long since elapsed, with an early option to lenders, either to receive back their money at the expiration of those periods, or to continue it at interest, till the whole amount of continental bills circulating should not exceed the sum in circulation at the time of each loan. This contingency, in the sense of the contract, never happened; and the presumption is, that the creditors preferred continuing their money indefinitely at interest to receiving it in a depreciated and depreciating state.

The other parts of it were chiefly for objects which ought to have been paid for at the time—that is, when the services were performed, or the supplies furnished; and were not accompanied with any contract for interest.

But by different acts of Government and Administration, concurred in by the creditors, these parts of the debt have been converted into a capital, bearing an interest of six percent per annum, but without any definite period of redemption. A portion of the Loan Office debt has been exchanged for new securities of that import; and the whole of it seems to have acquired that character after the expiration of the periods prefixed for repayment.

If this view of the subject be a just one, the capital of the debt of the United States may be considered in the light of an annuity at the rate of six percent per annum, redeemable at the pleasure of the Government by payment of the principal: for it seems to be a clear position, that, when a Government contracts a debt payable with interest, without any precise time being stipulated or understood for payment of the capital, that time is a matter of pure discretion with the Government, which is at liberty to consult its own convenience respecting it, taking care to pay the interest with punctuality.

Wherefore, as long as the United States should pay the interest of their debt, as it accrued, their creditors would have no right to demand the principal.

But with regard to the arrears of interest, the case is different. These are now due, and those to whom they are due, have a right to claim immediate payment. To say that it would be impracticable to comply, would not vary the nature of the right. Nor can this idea of impracticability be honorably carried further than to justify the proposition of a new contract, upon the basis of a commutation of that right for an equivalent. This equivalent, too, ought to be a real and fair one. And what other fair equivalent can be imagined for the detention of money, but a reasonable interest? Or what can be the standard of that interest, but the market rate, or the rate which the Government pays in ordinary cases?

From this view of the matter, which appears to be the accurate and true one, it will follow that the arrears of interest are entitled to an equal provision with the principal of the debt.

The result of the foregoing discussion is this: That there ought to be no discrimination between the original holders of the debt, and present possessors by purchase; that it is expedient there should be an assumption of the state debts by the Union; and that the arrears of interest should be provided for on an equal footing with the principal.

The next inquiry, in order, toward determining the nature of a proper provision, respects the quantum of the debt, and present rates of interest.

The debt of the Union is distinguishable into foreign and domestic.

The foreign debt, as stated in Schedule B, amounts to, principal . . . .$10,070,307.00 bearing an interest of four, and partly an interest of five percent. Arrears of interest to the last of December, 1789 . 1,640,071.62
  Making, together $11,710,378.62

The domestic debt may be subdivided into liquidated and unliquidated; principal and interest.

The principal of the liquidated part, as stated in Schedule C, amounts to . . . .$27,383,917.74 bearing an interest of six percent.

The arrears of interest, as stated in the Schedule D, to the end of 1790, amount to. 13,030,168.20
  Making, together. $40,414,085.94

This includes all that has been paid in indents (except what has come into the treasury of the United States), which, in the opinion of the Secretary, can be considered in no other light than as interest due.

The unliquidated part of the domestic debt, which consists chiefly of the continental bills of credit, is not ascertained, but may be estimated at 2,000,000 dollars.

These several sums constitute the whole of the debt of the United States, amounting together to $54,124,464.56.

That of the individual states is not equally well ascertained.

The Schedule E shows the extent to which it has been ascertained by returns, pursuant to the orders of the House of the 21st September last; but this not comprehending all the states, the residue must be estimated from less authentic information.

The Secretary, however, presumes that the total amount may be safely stated at twenty-five millions of dollars, principal and interest. The present rate of interest in the states' debt is, in general, the same with that of the domestic debt of the Union.

On the supposition that the arrears of interest ought to be provided for, on the same terms with the principal, the annual amount of the interest, which, at the existing rates, would be payable on the entire mass of the public debt, would be:

On the foreign debt, computing the interest on the principal, as it stands, and allowing four percent on the arrears of interest
$542,599.66
On the domestic debt, including that of states 4,044,845.15
Making, together $4,587,444.81

The interesting problem now occurs: Is it in the power of the United States, consistently with those prudential considerations which ought not to be overlooked, to make a provision equal to the purpose of funding the whole debt, at the rates of interest which it now bears, in addition to the sum which will be necessary for the current service of the Government?

The Secretary will not say that such a provision would exceed the abilities of the country, but he is clearly of opinion that to make it would require the extension of taxation to a degree and to objects which the true interest of the public creditors forbids. It is, therefore, to be hoped, and even to be expected, that they will cheerfully concur in such modifications of their claims, on fair and equitable principles, as will facilitate to the Government an arrangement substantial, durable, and satisfactory to the community. The importance of the last characteristic will strike every discerning mind. No plan, however flattering in appearance, to which it did not belong, could be truly entitled to confidence.

It will not be forgotten that exigencies may, erelong, arise, which would call for resources greatly beyond what is now deemed sufficient for the current service; and that, should the faculties of the country be exhausted, or even strained, to provide for the public debt, there could be less reliance on the sacredness of the provision. But while the Secretary yields to the force of these considerations, he does not lose sight of those fundamental principles of good faith which dictate that every practicable exertion ought to be made, scrupulously to fulfill the engagements of the Government; that no change in the rights of its creditors ought to be attempted without their voluntary consent; and that this consent ought to be voluntary in fact as well as in name.

Consequently, that every proposal of a change ought to be in the shape of an appeal to their reason and to their interest, not to their necessities. To this end it is requisite that a fair equivalent should be offered for what may be asked to be given up, and unquestionable security for the remainder. Without this, an alteration consistently with the credit and honor of the nation would be impracticable.

It remains to see what can be proposed in conformity to these views.

It has been remarked that the capital of the debt of the Union is to be viewed in the light of an annuity, at the rate of six percent per annum, redeemable at the pleasure of the Government by payment of the principal. And it will not be required that the arrears of interest should be considered in a more favorable light. The same character, in general, may be applied to the debts of the individual states.

This view of the subject admits that the United States would have it in their power to avail themselves of any fall in the market rate of interest for reducing that of the debt.

This property of the debt is favorable to the public, unfavorable to the creditor, and may facilitate an arrangement for the reduction of interest upon the basis of a fair equivalent.

Probabilities are always a rational ground of contract. The Secretary conceives that there is good reason to believe, if effectual measures are taken to establish public credit, that the Government rate of interest in the United States will, in a very short time, fall at least as low as five percent; and that, in a period not exceeding twenty years, it will sink still lower, probably to four. There are two principal causes which will be likely to produce this effect: one, the low rate of interest in Europe; the other, the increase of the moneyed capital of the nation by the funding of the public debt.

From three to four percent is deemed good interest in several parts of Europe. Even less is deemed so in some places; and it is on the decline, the increasing plenty of money continually tending to lower it. It is presumable, that no country will be able to borrow of foreigners upon better terms than the United States, because none can, perhaps, afford so good security. Our situation exposes us, less than that of any other nation, to those casualties which are the chief causes of expense; our encumbrances, in proportion to our real means, are less, though these cannot immediately be brought so readily into action; and our progress in resources, from the early state of the country, and the immense tracts of unsettled territory, must necessarily exceed that of any other. The advantages of this situation have already engaged the attention of the European money-lenders, particularly among the Dutch. And as they become better understood, they will have the greater influence. Hence, as large a proportion of the cash of Europe as may be wanted will be, in a certain sense, in our market, for the use of Government. And this will naturally have the effect of a reduction of the rate of interest, not indeed to the level of the places which send their money to market, but to something much nearer to it than our present rate.

The influence which the funding of the debt is calculated to have in lowering interest has been already remarked and explained. It is hardly possible that it should not be materially affected by such an increase of the moneyed capital of the nation as would result from the proper funding of seventy millions of dollars. But the probability of a decrease in the rate of interest acquires confirmation from facts which existed prior to the Revolution. It is well known that, in some of the states, money might, with facility, be borrowed, on good security, at five percent, and, not infrequently, even at less.

The most enlightened of the public creditors will be most sensible of the justness of this view of the subject, and of the propriety of the use which will be made of it.

The Secretary, in pursuance of it, will assume, as a probability sufficiently great to be a ground of calculation, both on the part of the Government and of its creditors, that the interest of money in the United States will, in five years, fall to five percent, and, in twenty, to four. The probability, in the mind of the Secretary, is rather that the fall may be more rapid and more considerable; but he prefers a mean, as most likely to engage the assent of the creditors, and more equitable in itself; because it is predicated on probabilities, which may err on one side as well as on the other.

Premising these things, the Secretary submits to the House the expediency of proposing a loan, to the full amount of the debt, as well of the particular states as of the Union, upon the following terms:

First—That, for every hundred dollars subscribed, payable in the debt (as well interest as principal), the subscriber be entitled, at his option, either

To have two thirds funded at an annuity or yearly interest of six percent, redeemable at the pleasure of the Government by payment of the principal, and to receive the other third in lands in the Western territory, at the rate of twenty cents per acre. Or,

To have the whole sum funded at an annuity or yearly interest of four percent, irredeemable by any payment exceeding five dollars per annum, on account both of principal and interest, and to receive, as a compensation for the reduction of interest, fifteen dollars and eighty cents, payable in lands, as in the preceding case. Or,

To have sixty-six dollars and two thirds of a dollar funded immediately, at an annuity or yearly interest of six percent, irredeemable by any payment exceeding four dollars and two thirds of a dollar per annum, on account both of principal and interest, and to have, at the end of ten years, twenty-six dollars and eighty-eight cents funded at the like interest and rate of redemption; or to have an annuity, for the remainder of life, upon the contingency of fixing to a given age, not less distant than ten years, computing interest at four percent. Or,

To have an annuity for the remainder of life, upon the contingency of the survivorship of the younger of two persons, computing interest in this case also at four percent.

In addition to the foregoing loan, payable wholly in the debt, the Secretary would propose that one should be opened for ten millions of dollars, on the following plan:

That, for every hundred dollars subscribed, payable one half in specie and the other half in debt (as well principal as interest), the subscriber be entitled to an annuity or yearly interest of five percent, irredeemable by any payment exceeding six dollars per annum, on account both of principal and interest.

The principles and operation of these different plans may now require explanation.

The first is simply a proposition for paying one third of the debt in land, and funding the other two thirds at the existing rate of interest and upon the same terms of redemption to which it is at present subject.

Here is no conjecture, no calculation of probabilities. The creditor is offered the advantage of making his interest principal, and he is asked to facilitate to the Government an effectual provision for his demands, by accepting a third part of them in land, at a fair valuation.

The general price at which the Western lands have been heretofore sold, has been a dollar per acre in public securities; but, at the time the principal purchases were made, these securities were worth, in the market, less than three shillings in the pound. The nominal price, therefore, would not be the proper standard, under present circumstances, nor would the precise specie value then given be a just rule; because, as the payments were to be made by installments, and the securities were, at the times of the purchases, extremely low, the probability of a moderate rise must be presumed to have been taken into the account. Twenty cents, therefore, seems to bear an equitable proportion to the two considerations of value at the time and likelihood of increase.

It will be understood that, upon this plan, the public retains the advantage of availing itself of any fall in the market rate of interest, for reducing that upon the debt; which is perfectly just, as no present sacrifice, either in the quantum of the principal, or in the rate of interest, is required from the creditor.

The inducement to the measure is, the payment of one third of the debt in land.

The second plan is grounded upon the supposition that interest, in five years, will fall to five percent; in fifteen more, to four. As the capital remains entire, but bearing an interest of four percent only, compensation is to be made to the creditor for the interest of two percent per annum for five years, and of one percent per annum for fifteen years, to commence at the distance of five years. The present value of these two sums or annuities, computed according to the terms of the supposition, is, by strict calculation, fifteen dollars and the seven hundred and ninety-two thousandth part of a dollar—a fraction less than the sum proposed.

The inducement to the measure here is, the reduction of interest to a rate more within the compass of a convenient provision, and the payment of the compensation in lands.

The inducements to the individual are, the accommodation afforded to the public; the high probability of a complete equivalent; the chance even of gain, should the rate of interest fall, either more speedily or in a greater degree than the calculation supposes. Should it fall to five percent sooner than five years, should it fall lower than five before the additional fifteen were expired, or should it fall below four previous to the payment of the debt, there would be, in each case, an absolute profit to the creditor. As his capital will remain entire, the value of it will increase with every decrease of the rate of interest.

The third plan proceeds upon the like supposition of a successive fall in the rate of interest, and upon that supposition offers an equivalent to the creditor: One hundred dollars, bearing an interest of six percent for five years, or five percent for fifteen years, and thenceforth of four percent (these being the successive rates of interest in the market), is equal to a capital of $122 and 510725 parts· bearing an interest of four percent, which, converted into a capital bearing a fixed rate of interest of six percent, is equal to $81 and 6738166 parts.[*]

The difference between sixty-six dollars and two thirds of a dollar (the sum to be funded immediately) and this last sum is $15 and 0172 parts, which, at six percent per annum, amounts, at the end of ten years, to $26 and 8755 parts—the sum to be funded at the expiration of that period.

It ought, however, to be acknowledged that this calculation does not make allowance for the principle of redemption, which the plan itself includes; upon which principle, the equivalent, in a capital of six percent, would be, by strict calculation, $87 and 50766 parts.

But there are two considerations which induce the Secretary to think that the one proposed would operate more equitably than this: One is, that it may not be very early in the power of the United States to avail themselves of the right of redemption reserved in the plan; the other is, that with regard to the part to be funded at the end of ten years, the principle of redemption is suspended during that time, and the full interest of six percent goes on improving at the same rate, which, for the last five years, will exceed the market rate of interest, according to the supposition.

The equivalent is regulated in this plan by the circumstance of fixing the rate of interest higher than it is supposed it will continue to be in the market, permitting only a gradual discharge of the debt, in an established proportion, and consequently pre-

---

[*] That is, $81.6738166.

venting advantage being taken of any decrease of interest below the stipulated rate.

Thus the true value of eighty-one dollars and sixty-seven cents, the capital proposed, considered as a perpetuity, and bearing six percent interest, when the market rate of interest was five percent, would be a small fraction more than ninety-eight dollars; when it was four percent, it would be one hundred and twenty-two dollars and fifty-one cents. But the proposed capital being subject to gradual redemption, it is evident that its value, in each case, would be somewhat less. Yet, from this may be perceived the manner in which a less capital, at a fixed rate of interest, becomes an equivalent for a greater capital, at a rate liable to variation and diminution.

It is presumable that those creditors who do not entertain a favorable opinion of property in Western lands will give a preference to this last mode of modelling the debt. The Secretary is sincere in affirming that, in his opinion, it will be likely to prove, *to the full*, as beneficial to the creditor as a provision for his debt upon its present terms.

It is not intended, in either case, to oblige the Government to redeem in the proportion specified, but to secure to it the right of doing so, to avoid the inconvenience of a perpetuity.

The fourth and fifth plans abandon the supposition which is the basis of the two preceding ones, and offer only four percent throughout.

The reason of this is, that the payment being deferred, there will be an accumulation of compound interest, in the intermediate period, against the public, which, without a very provident administration, would turn to its detriment, and the suspension of the burden would be too apt to beget a relaxation of efforts in the meantime. The measure, therefore, its object being temporary accommodation, could only be advisable upon a moderate rate of interest.

With regard to individuals, the inducement will be sufficient at four percent. There is no disposition of money, in private loans, making allowance for the usual delays and casualties, which would be equally beneficial as a future provision.

A hundred dollars advanced upon the life of a person of eleven years old would produce an annuity,

If commencing at twenty-one, of. . . . .$10 and 346 parts
If commencing at thirty-one, of. . . . . .$18 and 803 parts
If commencing at forty-one, of . . . . . .$37 and 286 parts
If commencing at fifty-one, of . . . .$78 and 580 parts

The same sum advanced upon the chance of the survivorship of the younger of two lives, one of the persons being twenty-five, the other thirty years old, would produce, if the younger of the two should survive, an annuity for the remainder of life, of twenty-three dollars, five hundred and fifty-six parts.

From these instances may readily be discerned the advantages which these deferred annuities afford, for securing a comfortable provision for the evening of life, or for wives who survive their husbands.

The sixth plan also relinquishes the supposition, which is the foundation of the second and third, and offers a higher rate of interest, upon similar terms of redemption, for the consideration of the payment of one half of the loan in specie. This is a plan highly advantageous to the creditors who may be able to make that payment, while the specie itself could be applied in purchases of the debt, upon terms which would fully indemnify the public for the increased interest.

It is not improbable that foreign holders of the domestic debt may embrace this as a desirable arrangement.

As an auxiliary expedient, and by way of experiment, the Secretary would propose a loan upon the principles of a tontine—

To consist of six classes, composed respectively of persons of the following ages:

First class, of those of 20 years and under.

Second class, of those above 20, and not exceeding 30.

Third class, of those above 30, and not exceeding 40.

Fourth class, of those above 40, and not exceeding 50.

Fifth class, of those above 50, and not exceeding 60.

Sixth class, of those above 60.

Each share to be two hundred dollars; the number of shares in each class to be indefinite. Persons to be at liberty to subscribe on their own lives, or on those of others nominated by them.

The annuity upon a share in the first class, to be . . $ 8.40
Upon a share in the second $8.65
Upon a share in the third $9.00
Upon a share in the fourth $9.65
Upon a share in the fifth $10.70
Upon a share in the sixth $12.80

The annuities of those who die to be equally divided among the survivors, until four fifths shall be dead, when the principle of survivorship shall cease, and each annuitant thenceforth enjoy his dividend as a several annuity during the life upon which it shall depend.

These annuities are calculated on the best life in each class, and at a rate of interest of four percent, with some deductions in favor of the public. To the advantages which these circumstances present, the cessation of the right of survivorship, on the death of four fifths of the annuitants, will be no inconsiderable addition.

The inducements to individuals are, a competent interest for their money from the outset, secured for life, with a prospect of continual increase, and even of a large profit to those whose fortune it is to survive their associates.

It will have appeared that, in all the proposed loans, the Secretary has contemplated the putting the interest upon the same footing with the principal. *That* on the debt of the United States, he would have computed to the last of the present year; *that* on the debt of the particular states, to the last of the year 1791; the reason for which distinction will be seen hereafter.

In order to keep up a due circulation of money, it will be expedient that the interest of the debt should be paid quarter-yearly. This regulation will, at the same time, conduce to the advantage of the public creditors, giving them, in fact, by the anticipation of payment, a higher rate of interest; which may, with propriety, be taken into the estimate of the compensation to be made to them. Six percent per annum, paid in this mode, will truly be worth six dollars and the one hundred and thirty-five thousandth part of a dollar, computing the market interest at the same rate.

The Secretary thinks it advisable to hold out various propositions, all of them compatible with the public interest, because it is, in his opinion, of the greatest consequence that the debt should, with the consent of the creditors, be remolded into such a shape as will bring the expenditure of the nation to a level with its income. Till this shall be accomplished the finances of the United States will never wear a proper countenance. Arrears of interest, continually accruing, will be as continual a monument, either of inability or of ill faith, and will not cease to have an evil influence on public credit. In nothing are appearances of greater moment than in whatever regards credit. Opinion is the soul of it; and this is affected by appearances as well as realities. By offering an option to the creditors between a number of plans, the change meditated will be more likely to be accomplished. Different tempers will be governed by different views of the subject.

But while the Secretary would endeavor to effect a change in the form of the debt by new loans, in order to render it more susceptible of an adequate provision, he would not think it proper to aim at procuring the concurrence of the creditors by operating upon their necessities.

Hence, whatever surplus of revenue might remain, after satisfying the interest of the new loans and the demand for the current service, ought to be divided among those creditors, if any, who may not think fit to subscribe to them. But for this purpose, under the circumstance of depending propositions, a temporary appropriation will be most advisable, and the sum must be limited to four percent, as the revenues will only be calculated to produce in that proportion to the entire debt.

The Secretary confides, for the success of the propositions to be made, on the goodness of the reasons upon which they rest;

on the fairness of the equivalent to be offered in each case; on the discernment of the creditors of their true interest, and on their disposition to facilitate the arrangements of the Government, and to render them satisfactory to the community.

The remaining part of the task to be performed is to take a view of the means of providing for the debt, according to the modification of it which is proposed.

On this point the Secretary premises that, in his opinion, the funds to be established ought, for the present, to be confined to the existing debt of the United States; as well because the progressive augmentation of the revenue will be most convenient, as because the consent of the state creditors is necessary to the assumption contemplated; and though the obtaining of that consent may be inferred with great assurance from their obvious interest to give it, yet, till it shall be obtained, an actual provision for the debt would be premature. Taxes could not, with propriety, be laid for an object which depended on such a contingency.

All that ought now to be done respecting it is to put the matter in an effectual train for a future provision. For which purpose the Secretary will, in the course of this report, submit such propositions as appear to him advisable.

The Secretary now proceeds to a consideration of the necessary funds.

It has been stated that the debt of the United States consists of the foreign debt, amounting, with arrears of interest, to

$11,710,378.62

And the domestic debt, amounting, with like arrears, computed to the end of the year 1790, to......... 42,414,085.94

Making, together.................... $54,124,464.56

The interest on the domestic debt is computed to the end of this year, because the details of carrying any plan into execution will exhaust the year.

The annual interest of the foreign debt has been stated at

$542,599.66

And the interest on the domestic debt, at four percent, would amount to 1,696,563.43

Making, together $2,239,163.09

Thus, to pay the interest of the foreign debt, and to pay four percent on the whole of the domestic debt, principal and interest, forming a new capital, will require a yearly income of $2,239,163.09

The sum which, in the opinion of the Secretary, ought now to be provided, in addition to what the current service will require.

For, though the rate of interest proposed by the third plan exceeds four percent on the whole debt and the annuities on the tontine will also exceed four percent on the sums which may be subscribed; yet, as the actual provision for a part is in the former case suspended, as measures for reducing the debt by purchases may be advantageously pursued, and as the payment of the deferred annuities will of course be postponed, four percent on the whole will be a sufficient provision.

With regard to the installments of the foreign debt, these, in the opinion of the Secretary, ought to be paid by new loans abroad. Could funds be conveniently spared from other exigencies for paying them, the United States could illy bear the drain of cash, at the present juncture, which the measure would be likely to occasion.

But to the sum which has been stated for payment of the interest must be added a provision for the current service. This the Secretary estimates at six hundred thousand dollars; making, with the amount of the interest, two millions eight hundred and thirty-nine thousand one hundred and sixty-three dollars and nine cents.

This sum may, in the opinion of the Secretary, be obtained from the present duties on imports and tonnage, with the additions which, without any possible disadvantage, either to trade or agriculture, may be made on wines, spirits (including those distilled within the United States), teas, and coffee.

The Secretary conceives that it will be sound policy to carry the duties upon articles of this kind as high as will be consistent with the practicability of a safe collection. This will lessen the necessity, both of having recourse to direct taxation, and of accumulating duties where they would be more inconvenient to trade and upon objects which are more to be regarded as necessaries of life.

That the articles which have been enumerated will, better than most others, bear high duties, can hardly be a question. They are all of them in reality luxuries; the greatest part of them foreign luxuries; some of them, in the excess in which they are used, pernicious luxuries. And there is, perhaps, none of them which is not consumed in so great abundance as may justly denominate it a source of national extravagance and impoverishment. The consumption of ardent spirits, particularly, no doubt very much on account of their cheapness, is carried to an extreme which is truly to be regretted, as well in regard to the health and morals as to the economy of the community.

Should the increase of duties tend to a decrease of the consumption of those articles, the effect would be in every respect desirable. The saving which it would occasion would leave individuals more at their ease, and promote a favorable balance of trade. As far as this decrease might be applicable to distilled spirits, it would encourage the substitution of cider and malt liquors, benefit agriculture, and open a new and productive source of revenue.

It is not, however, probable that this decrease would be in a degree which would frustrate the expected benefit to the revenue from raising the duties. Experience has shown that luxuries of every kind lay the strongest hold on the attachments of mankind, which, especially when confirmed by habit, are not easily alienated from them.

The same fact affords a security to the merchant that he is not likely to be prejudiced by considerable duties on such articles. They will usually command a proportional price. The chief things, in this view, to be attended to, are, that the terms of payment be so regulated as not to require inconvenient advances, and that the mode of collection be secure.

To other reasons, which plead for carrying the duties upon the articles which have been mentioned, to as great an extent as they will bear, may be added these: that they are of a nature, from their extensive consumption, to be very productive, and are amongst the most difficult objects of illicit introduction.

Invited by so many motives to make the best use of the resource which these articles afford, the essential inquiry is, in what mode can the duties upon them be most effectually collected?

With regard to such of them as will be brought from abroad, a duty on importation recommends itself by two leading considerations: one is, that, meeting the object at its first entrance into the country, the collection is drawn to a point, and, so far, simplified; the other is, that it avoids the possibility of interference between the regulations of the United States and those of the particular states.

But a duty, the precautions for the collection of which should terminate with the landing of the goods, as is essentially the case in the existing system, could not, with safety, be carried to the extent which is contemplated.

In that system, the evasion of the duty depends, as it were, on a single risk. To land the goods in defiance of the vigilance of the officers of the customs, is almost the sole difficulty. No future pursuit is materially to be apprehended. And where the inducement is equivalent to the risk, there will be found too many who are willing to run it. Consequently, there will be extensive frauds of the revenue, against which the utmost rigor of penal laws has proved, as often as it has been tried, an ineffectual guard.

The only expedient which has been discovered, for conciliating high duties with a safe collection, is the establishment of a second or interior scrutiny.

By pursuing the article, from its importation into the hands of the dealers in it, the risk of detection is so greatly enhanced, that few, in comparison, will venture to incur it. Indeed, every dealer who is not himself the fraudulent importer, then becomes in some sort a sentinel upon him.

The introduction of a system founded on this principle in some shape or other, is, in the opinion of the Secretary, essential to the efficacy of every attempt to render the revenues of the United States equal to their exigencies, their safety, their prosperity, their honor.

Nor is it less essential to the interest of the honest and fair trader. It might even be added, that every individual citizen, besides his share in the general weal, has a particular interest in it. The practice of smuggling never fails to have one of two effects, and sometimes unites them both. Either the smuggler undersells the fair trader, as, by saving the duty, he can afford to do, and makes it a charge upon him, or he sells at the increased price occasioned by the duty, and defrauds every man who buys of him, of his share of what the public ought to receive; for it is evident that the loss falls ultimately upon the citizens, who must be charged with other taxes to make good the deficiency and supply the wants of the State.

The Secretary will not presume that the plan which he shall submit to the consideration of the House is the best that could be devised. But it is the one which has appeared to him freest from objections, of any that has occurred, of equal efficacy. He acknowledges, too, that it is susceptible of improvement, by other precautions in favor of the revenue, which he did not think it expedient to add. The chief outlines of the plan are not original; but it is no ill recommendation of it, that it has been tried with success.

The Secretary accordingly proposes,

That the duties heretofore laid upon wines, distilled spirits, teas, and coffee, should, after the last day of May next, cease; and that, instead of them, the following duties be laid:

Upon every gallon of Madeira wine, the quality of London particular, thirty-five cents.

Upon every gallon of other Madeira wine, thirty cents.

Upon every gallon of Sherry, twenty-five cents.

Upon every gallon of other wine, twenty cents.

Upon every gallon of distilled spirits more than ten percent below proof, according to Dicas' hydrometer, twenty cents.

Upon every gallon of those spirits under five and not more than ten percent below proof, according to the same hydrometer, twenty-one cents.

Upon every gallon of those spirits, of proof, and not more than five percent below proof, according to the same hydrometer, twenty-two cents.

Upon every gallon of those spirits, above proof, but not exceeding twenty percent according to the same hydrometer, twenty-five cents.

Upon every gallon of those spirits, more than twenty, and not more than forty percent above proof, according to the same hydrometer, thirty cents.

Upon every gallon of those spirits, more than forty percent above proof, according to the same hydrometer, forty cents.

Upon every pound of Hyson tea, forty cents.

Upon every pound of other green tea, twenty-four cents.

Upon every pound of Souchong and other black teas, except Bohea, twenty cents.

Upon every pound of Bohea tea, twelve cents.

Upon every pound of coffee, five cents.

That, upon spirits distilled within the United States, from molasses, sugar, or other foreign materials, there be paid:

Upon every gallon of those spirits, more than ten percent below proof, according to Dicas' hydrometer, eleven cents.

Upon every gallon of those spirits, under five, and not more than ten percent below proof, according to the same hydrometer, twelve cents.

Upon every gallon of those spirits, of proof, and not more than five percent below proof, according to the same hydrometer, thirteen cents.

Upon every gallon of those spirits, above proof, but not exceeding twenty percent according to the same hydrometer, fifteen cents.

Upon every gallon of those spirits, more than twenty, and not more than forty percent above proof, according to the same hydrometer, twenty cents.

Upon every gallon of those spirits, more than forty percent above proof, according to the same hydrometer, thirty cents.

That, upon spirits distilled within the United States, in any city, town, or village, from materials of the growth or production of the United States, there be paid:

Upon every gallon of those spirits, more than ten percent below proof, according to Dicas' hydrometer, nine cents.

Upon every gallon of those spirits, under five, and not more than ten percent below proof, according to the same hydrometer, ten cents.

Upon every gallon of those spirits, of proof, and not more than five percent below proof, according to the same hydrometer, eleven cents.

Upon every gallon of those spirits, above proof, but not exceeding twenty percent according to the same hydrometer, thirteen cents.

Upon every gallon of those spirits, more than twenty, and not more than forty percent above proof, according to the same hydrometer, seventeen cents.

Upon every gallon of those spirits, more than forty percent above proof, according to the same hydrometer, twenty-five cents.

That, upon all stills employed in distilling spirits from materials of the growth or production of the United States, in any other place than a city, town, or village, there be paid the yearly sum of sixty cents, for every gallon, English wine measure, of the capacity of each still, including its head.

The Secretary does not distribute the duties on teas into different classes, as has been done in the impost act of the last session; because this distribution depends on considerations of commercial policy, not of revenue. It is sufficient, therefore, for him to remark, that the rates above specified are proposed with reference to the lowest class.

The Secretary, conceiving that he could not convey an accurate idea of the plan contemplated by him, for the collection of these duties, in any mode so effectual as by the draught of a bill for the purpose, begs leave, respectfully, to refer the House to that which will be found annexed to this report, relatively to the article of distilled spirits; and which, for the better explanation of some of its parts, is accompanied with marginal remarks.

It would be the intention of the Secretary that the duty on wines should be collected upon precisely the same plan with that on imported spirits.

But, with regard to teas and coffee, the Secretary is inclined to think that it will be expedient, till experience shall evince the propriety of going further, to exclude the ordinary right of the officers to visit and inspect the places in which those articles may be kept. The other precautions, without this, will afford, though not complete, considerable security.

It will not escape the observation of the House that the Secretary, in the plan submitted, has taken the most scrupulous care that those citizens upon whom it is immediately to operate, be secured from every species of injury by the misconduct of the officers to be employed. There are not only strong guards against their being guilty of abuses of authority; they are not only punishable, criminally, for any they may commit, and made answerable in damages, to individuals, for whatever prejudice these may sustain by their acts or neglects; but even where seizures are made with probable cause, if there be an acquittal of the articles seized a compensation to the proprietors for the injury their property may suffer, and even for its detention, is to be made out of the public treasury.

So solicitous, indeed, has the Secretary been to obviate every appearance of hardship, that he has even included a compensation to the dealers for their agency in aid of the revenue.

With all these precautions to manifest a spirit of moderation and justice on the part of the Government; and when it is considered that the object of the proposed system is the firm establishment of public credit; that, on this depends the character, security, and prosperity of the nation; that advantages, in every light important, may be expected to result from it; that the immediate operation of it will be upon an enlightened class of citizens, zealously devoted to good government, and to a liberal and enlarged policy; and that it is peculiarly the interest of the virtuous part of them to co-operate in whatever will restrain the spirit of illicit traffic; there will be perceived to exist the justest ground of confidence that the plan, if eligible in itself, will experience the cheerful and prompt acquiescence of the community.

The Secretary computes the net product of the duties proposed in this report at about one million seven hundred and three thousand four hundred dollars, according to the estimate in Schedule K, which, if near the truth, will, together with the probable product of the duties on imposts and tonnage, complete the sum required. But it will readily occur, that in so unexplored a field there must be a considerable degree of uncertainty in the data; and that on this account it will be prudent to have an auxiliary resource for the first year in which the interest will become payable, that there may be no possibility of disappointment to the public creditors ere there may be an opportunity of providing for any deficiency which the experiment may discover. This will, accordingly, be attended to.

The proper appropriation of the funds provided and to be provided seems next to offer itself to consideration.

On this head, the Secretary would propose that the duties on distilled spirits should be applied, in the first instance, to the payment of the interest on the foreign debt.

That, reserving out of the residue of those duties an annual sum of six hundred thousand dollars for the current service of the United States, the surplus, together with the product of the other duties, be applied to the payment of the interest on the new loan, by an appropriation coextensive with the duration of the debt.

And that, if any part of the debt should remain unsubscribed, the excess of the revenue be divided among the creditors of the unsubscribed part by a temporary disposition, with a limitation, however, to four percent.

It will hardly have been unnoticed that the Secretary has been, thus far, silent on the subject of the Post Office. The reason is, that he has had in view the application of the revenue arising from that source to the purpose of a sinking fund. The Postmaster-General gives it as his opinion that the immediate product of it, upon a proper arrangement, would probably be not less than one hundred thousand dollars. And, from its nature, with good management, it must be a growing, and will be likely to become, a considerable fund. The Postmaster-General is now engaged in preparing a plan which will be the foundation of a proposition for a new arrangement of the establishment. This, and some other points relative to the subject referred to the Secretary, he begs leave to reserve for a future report.

Persuaded, as the Secretary is, that the proper funding of the present debt will render it a national blessing, yet he is so far from acceding to the position, in the latitude in which it is sometimes laid down, that "public debts are public benefits"—a position inviting to prodigality and liable to dangerous abuse—that he ardently wishes to see it incorporated as a fundamental maxim in the system of public credit of the United States, that the creation of debt should always be accompanied with the means of extinguishment. This he regards as the true secret for rendering public credit immortal. And he presumes that it is difficult to conceive a situation in which there may not be an adherence to the maxim. At least, he feels an unfeigned solicitude that this may be attempted by the United States, and that they may commence their measures for the establishment of credit with the observance of it.

Under this impression, the Secretary proposes that the net product of the Post Office to a sum not exceeding one million of dollars be vested in commissioners, to consist of the Vice-President of the United States, or President of the Senate, the Speaker of the House of Representatives, the Chief Justice, Secretary of the Treasury, and Attorney-General of the United States, for the time being, in trust; to be applied by them, or any three of them, to the discharge of the existing public debt, either by purchases of stock in the market, or by payments on account of the principal, as shall appear to them most advisable, in conformity to public engagements; to continue so vested until the whole of the debt shall be discharged.

As an additional expedient for effecting a reduction of the debt, and for other purposes, which will be mentioned, the Secretary would further propose, that the same commissioners be authorized, with the approbation of the President of the United States, to borrow, on their credit, a sum not exceeding twelve millions of dollars, to be applied:

First. To the payment of the interest and installments of the foreign debt, to the end of the present year, which will require 3,491,932 dollars and 46 cents.

Secondly. To the payment of any deficiency which may happen in the product of the funds provided for paying the interest of the domestic debt.

Thirdly. To the effecting a change in the form of such part of the foreign debt as bears an interest of five percent. It is conceived that for this purpose a new loan at a lower interest may be combined with other expedients. The remainder of this part of the debt, after paying the installments which will accrue in the course of 1790, will be 3,888,888 dollars and 81 cents.

Fourthly. To purchase of the public debt, at the price it shall bear in the market, while it continues below its true value. This measure, which would be, in the opinion of the Secretary, highly dishonorable to the Government if it were to precede a provision for funding the debt, would become altogether unexceptionable after that had been made. Its effect would be in favor of the public creditors, as it would tend to raise the value of stock; and all the difference between its true value and the actual price would be so much clear gain to the public. The payment of foreign interest on the capital to be borrowed for this purpose, should that be a necessary consequence, would not, in the judgment of the Secretary, be a good objection to the measure. The saving, by the operation, would be itself a sufficient indemnity; and the employment of that capital, in a country situated like this, would much more than compensate for it. Besides, if the Government does not undertake this operation, the same inconvenience which the objection in question supposes, would happen in another way, with a circumstance of aggravation. As long, at least, as the debt shall continue below its proper value it will be an object of speculation to foreigners, who will not only receive the interest upon what they purchase, and remit it abroad, as in the case of the loan, but will reap the additional profit of the difference in value. By the Government's entering into competition with them, it will not only reap a part of the profit itself, but will contract the extent, and lessen the extra profit of foreign purchases. That competition will accelerate the rise of stock; and whatever greater rate this obliges foreigners to pay for what they purchase, is so much clear saving to the nation. In the opinion of the Secretary, and contrary to an idea which is not without patrons, it ought to be the policy of the Government to raise the value of stock to its true standard as fast as possible. When it arrives to that point, foreign speculations (which, till then, must be deemed pernicious, further than as they serve to bring it to that point) will become beneficial. Their money, laid out in this country upon our agriculture, commerce, and manufactures, will produce much more to us than the income they will receive from it.

The Secretary contemplates the application of this money through the medium of a national bank, for which, with the permission of the House, he will submit a plan in the course of the session.

The Secretary now proceeds, in the last place, to offer to the consideration of the House his ideas of the steps which ought, at the present session, to be taken toward the assumption of the state debts.

These are, briefly, that concurrent resolutions of the two Houses, with the approbation of the President be entered into, declaring in substance:

That the United States do assume, and will, at the first session in the year 1791, provide, on the same terms with the present debt of the United States, for all such parts of the debts of the respective states, or any of them, as shall, prior to the first day of January, in the said year, 1791, be subscribed toward a loan to the United States, upon the principles of either of the plans which shall have been adopted by them, for obtaining a reloan of their present debt.

Provided, that the provision to be made, as aforesaid, shall be suspended, with respect to the debt of any state which may have exchanged the securities of the United States for others issued by itself, until the whole of the said securities shall either be re-exchanged or surrendered to the United States.

And provided, also, that the interest upon the debt assumed, be computed to the end of the year 1791; and that the interest to be paid by the United States commence on the first day of January, 1792.

That the amount of the debt of each state, so assumed and provided for, be charged to such state in account with the United States, upon the same principles upon which it shall be lent to the United States.

That subscriptions be opened for receiving loans of the said debts, at the same times and places, and under the like regulations, as shall have been prescribed in relation to the debt of the United States.

The Secretary has now completed the objects which he proposed to himself to comprise in the present report. He has for the most part omitted details, as well to avoid fatiguing the attention of the House as because more time would have been desirable, even to digest the general principles of the plan. If these should be found right, the particular modifications will readily suggest themselves in the progress of the work.

The Secretary, in the views which have directed his pursuit of the subject, has been influenced, in the first place, by the consideration that his duty, from the very terms of the resolution of the House, obliged him to propose what appeared to him an adequate provision for the support of the public credit, adapted at the same time to the real circumstances of the United States; and, in the next, by the reflection that measures which will not bear the test of future unbiassed examination, can neither be productive of individual reputation nor (which is of much greater consequence) public honor or advantage.

Deeply impressed, as the Secretary is, with a full and deliberate conviction that the establishment of the public credit, upon the basis of a satisfactory provision for the public debt, is, under the present circumstances of this country, the true desideratum toward relief from individual and national embarrassments; that without it these embarrassments will be likely to press still more severely upon the community; he cannot but indulge an anxious wish that an effectual plan for that purpose may during the present session be the result of the united wisdom of the Legislature.

He is fully convinced that it is of the greatest importance that no further delay should attend the making of the requisite provision; not only because it will give a better impression of the good faith of the country, and will bring earlier relief to the creditors, both which circumstances are of great moment to public credit, but because the advantages to the community, from raising stock, as speedily as possible, to its natural value, will be incomparably greater than any that can result from its continuance below that standard. No profit which could be derived from purchases in the market, on account of the Government, to any practicable extent, would be an equivalent for the loss which would be sustained by the purchases of foreigners at a low value. Not to repeat, that governmental purchases to be honorable ought to be preceded by a provision. Delay, by disseminating doubt, would sink the price of stock; and, as the temptation to foreign speculations, from the lowness of the price, would be too great to be neglected, millions would probably be lost to the United States.

All of which is humbly submitted.

Alexander Hamilton,

    Secretary of the Treasury.

To this report were appended several schedules:

A. Being a suppositious statement of accounts between the United States and individual states.

B. A general statement of the Foreign Loans, showing, in abstract, the capital sums borrowed, and the arrearages of interest, to the 31st of December, 1789.

C. Abstract of the Liquidated and Loan-Office Debt of the United States, on the 3d of March, 1789.

D. An estimate of all the interest which will accrue on the Domestic Debt of the United States, from its formation to 31st of December, 1790; of such partial payments as have been made on account thereof, and of the balance which will remain to be provided for, to pay up the interest fully to that period.

E. Abstract of the public debt of the states (therein) mentioned agreeably to accounts transmitted in pursuance of the resolution of the House of Representatives of the 21st of September, 1789.

F. Table, showing the annuity which a person of a given age would be entitled to, during life, from the time he should arrive at a given age, upon the present payment of a hundred dollars, computing interest at four percent.

G. Table, showing what annuity would be enjoyed by the survivor of only two persons, of certain ages, for the remainder of life, after the determination of life in expectation, upon the present payment of one hundred dollars, computing interest at four percent per annum, and the duration of life, according to Dr. Halley's tables.

H. Table for a Tontine of Six Classes, the number of lives in each Class being indefinite, calculated on a payment of two hundred dollars by each subscriber, and at a rate of interest of four percent. The computation on the best life in each Class, and on the supposition that the subscribers to each Class will not be less than the respective numbers specified in the first column.

I. General Estimate for the services of the current year.

K. Estimate of the probable product of the funds proposed for funding the debt, and providing for the current service of the United States, including the present duties on imports and tonnage.

The Second Report on the Further Provision Necessary for Establishing Public Credit (The Report on a National Bank)

December 1790

To the Speaker of the House of Representatives:

In obedience to the order of the House of Representatives of the ninth day of August last, requiring the Secretary of the Treasury to prepare and report on this day such further provision as may, in his opinion, be necessary for establishing the public Credit.

The said Secretary further respectfully reports

That from a conviction (as suggested in his report No. 1 herewith presented) that a National Bank is an Institution of primary importance to the prosperous administration of the Finances, and would be of the greatest utility in the operations connected with the support of the Public Credit, his attention has been drawn to devising the plan of such an institution, upon a scale which will entitle it to the confidence, and be likely to render it equal to the exigencies of the Public.

Previously to entering upon the detail of this plan, he entreats the indulgence of the House, towards some preliminary reflections naturally arising out of the subject, which he hopes will be deemed, neither useless, nor out of place. Public opinion being the ultimate arbiter of every measure of Government, it can scarcely appear improper, in deference to that, to accompany the origination of any new proposition with explanations, which the superior information of those, to whom it is immediately addressed, would render superfluous.

It is a fact well understood, that public Banks have found admission and patronage among the principal and most enlightened commercial nations. They have successively obtained in Italy, Germany, Holland, England and France, as well as in the United States. And it is a circumstance, which cannot but have considerable weight in a candid estimate of their tendency, that after an experience of centuries, there exists not a question about their utility in the countries in which they have been so long established. Theories and men of business unite in the acknowledgement of it.

Trade and industry, wherever they have been tried, have been indebted to them for important aid. And Government has been repeatedly under the greatest obligations to them, in dangerous and distressing emergencies. That of the United States, as well in some of the most critical conjunctures of the late war, as since the peace has received assistance from those established among us, with which it could not have dispensed.

With this two fold evidence before us, it might be expected, that there would be a perfect union of opinions in their favor. Yet doubts have been entertained; jealousies and prejudices have circulated: and though the experiment is every day dissipating them within the spheres in which effects are best known; yet there are still persons by whom they have not been entirely renounced. To give a full and accurate view of the subject would be to make a Treatise of a report; but there are certain aspects in which it may be cursorily exhibited, which may perhaps conduce to a just impression of its merits. These will involve a comparison of the advantages, with the disadvantages, real or supposed, of such institutions.

The following are among the principal advantages of a Bank.

First. The augmentation of the active or productive capital of a country. Gold and Silver, when they are employed merely as the instruments of exchange and alienation, have been not improperly denominated dead Stock; but when deposited in Banks, to become the basis of a paper circulation, which takes their character and place, as the signs or representatives of value, they then acquire life, or, in other words, an active and productive quality. This idea, which appears rather subtle and abstract, in a general form, may be made obvious and palpable, by entering into a few particulars. It is evident, for instance, that the money, which a merchant keeps in his chest, waiting for a favorable opportunity to employ it, produces nothing 'till that opportunity arrives. But if instead of locking it up in this manner, he either deposits it in a Bank, or invests it in the Stock of a Bank, it yields a profit, during the interval; in which he partakes, or not, according to the choice he may have made of being a depositor or a proprietor; and when any advantageous speculation offers, in order to be able to embrace it, he has only to withdraw his money, if a depositor, or if a proprietor to obtain a loan from the Bank, or to dispose of his Stock; an alternative seldom or never attended with difficulty, when the affairs of the institution are in a prosperous train. His money thus deposited or invested, is a fund, upon which himself and others can borrow to a much larger amount. It is a well established fact, that Banks in good credit can circulate a far greater sum than the actual quantum of their capital in Gold and Silver. The extent of the possible excess seems indeterminate; though it has been conjecturally stated at the proportions of two and three to one. This faculty is produced in various ways. First. A great proportion of the notes, which are issued and pass current as Cash, are indefinitely suspended in circulation, from the confidence which each holder has, that he can at any moment turn them into gold and silver. Secondly, Every loan, which a Bank makes is, in its first shape, a credit given to the borrower on its books, the amount of which it stands ready to pay, either in its own notes, or in gold or silver, at his option. But, in a great number of cases, no actual payment is made in either. The Borrower frequently, by a check or order, transfers his credit to some other person, to whom he has a payment to make; who, in his turn, is as often content with a similar credit, because he is satisfied, that he can, whenever he pleases, either convert it into cash, or pass it to some other hand, as an equivalent for it. And in this manner the credit keeps circulating, performing in every stage the office of money, till it is extinguished by a discount with some person, who has a payment to make to the Bank, to an equal or greater amount. Thus large sums are lent and paid, frequently through a variety of hands, without the intervention of a single piece of coin. Thirdly, There is always a large quantity of gold and silver in the repositories of the Bank, besides its own Stock, which is placed there, with a view partly to its safe keeping and partly to the accommodation of an institution, which is itself a source of general accommodation. These deposits are of immense consequence in the operations of a Bank. Though liable to be redrawn at any moment, experience proves, that the money so much oftener changes proprietors than place, and that what is drawn out is generally so speedily replaced as to authorise the counting upon the sums deposited, as an *effective fund*; which, concurring with the Stock of the Bank, enables it to extend its loans, and to answer all the demands for coin, whether in consequence of those loans, or arising from the occasional return of its notes.

These different circumstances explain the manner, in which the ability of a bank to circulate a greater sum, than its actual capital in coin, is acquired. This however must be gradual; and must be preceded by a firm establishment of confidence; a confidence which may be bestowed on the most rational grounds; since the excess in question will always be bottomed on good security of one kind or another. This, every well conducted Bank carefully requires, before it will consent to advance either its money or its credit; and when there is an auxiliary capital (as will be the case in the plan hereafter submitted) which, together with the capital in coin, define the boundary, that shall not be exceeded by the engagements of the Bank, the security may, consistently with all the maxims of a reasonable circumspection be regarded as complete.

The same circumstances illustrate the truth of the position, that it is one of the properties of Banks to increase the active capital of a country. This, in other words is the sum of them. The money of one individual, while he is waiting for an opportunity to employ it by being either deposited in the Bank for safe keeping, or invested in its Stock, is in a condition to administer to the wants of others without being put out of his own reach, when occasion presents. This yields an extra profit, arising from what is paid for the use of his money by others, when he could not himself make use of it and keeps the money itself in a state of incessant activity, in the almost infinite vicissitudes and competitions of mercantile enterprise, there never can be danger of an intermission of demand, or that the money will remain for a moment idle in the vaults of the Bank. This additional employment given to money, and the faculty of a bank to lend and circulate a greater sum than the amount of its stock in coin are to all the purposes of trade and industry an absolute increase of capital. Purchases and undertakings, in general, can be carried on by any given sum of bank paper or credit, as effectually as by an equal sum of gold and silver. And thus by contributing to enlarge the mass of industrious and commercial enterprise, banks become nurseries of national wealth: a consequence, as satisfactorily verified by experience, as it is clearly deducible in theory.

Secondly, Greater facility to the Government in obtaining pecuniary aids, especially in sudden emergencies. This is another and an undisputed advantage of public banks: one, which as already remarked, has been realized in signal instances, among ourselves. The reason is obvious: The capitals of a great number of individuals are, by this operation, collected to a point, and placed under one direction. The mass, formed by this union, is in a certain sense magnified by the credit attached to it: And while this mass is always ready, and can at once be put in motion, in aid of the Government, the interest of the bank to afford that aid, independent of regard to the public safety and welfare, is a sure pledge for its disposition to go as far in its compliances, as can in prudence be desired. There is in the nature of things, as will be more particularly noticed in another place, an intimate connection of interest between the government and the Bank of a Nation.

Thirdly. The facilitating of the payment of taxes. This advantage is produced in two ways. Those who are in a situation to have access to the Bank can have the assistance of loans to answer with punctuality the public calls upon them. This accommodation has been sensibly felt in the payment of the duties heretofore laid, by those who reside where establishments of this nature exist. This however, though an extensive, is not a universal benefit. The other way, in which the effect here contemplated is produced, and in which the benefit is general, is the increasing of the quantity of circulating medium and the quickening of circulation. The manner in which the first happens has already been traced. The last may require some illustration. When payments are to be made between different places, having an intercourse of business with each other, if there happen to be no private bills, at market, and there are no Bank notes, which have a currency in both, the consequence is, the coin must be remitted. This is attended with trouble, delay, expense and risk. If on the contrary, there are bank notes current in these places, the transmission of these by the post, or any other speedy, and convenient conveyance answers the purpose; and these again, in the alternations of demand, are frequently returned, very soon after, to the place from whence they were first sent: Whence the transportation and retransportation of the metals are obviated; and a more convenient and more expeditious medium of payment is substituted. Nor is this all. The metals, instead of being suspended from their usual functions, during this process of vibration from place to place continue in activity, and administer still to the ordinary circulation; which of course is prevented from suffering either diminution or stagnation. These circumstances are additional causes of what, in a practical sense or to the purposes of business, may be called greater plenty of money. And it is evident, that whatever enhances the quantity of circulating money adds to the ease, with which every industrious member of the community may acquire that portion of it, of which he stands in need; and enables him the better to pay his taxes, as well as to supply his other wants. Even where the circulation of the bank paper is not general, it must still have the same effect, though in a less degree. For whatever furnishes additional supplies to the channels of circulation, in one quarter, naturally contributes to keep the stream fuller elsewhere. This last view of the subject serves both to demonstrate the position, that Banks tend to facilitate the payment of taxes; and to exemplify their utility to business of every kind in which money is an agent.

It would be to intrude too much on the patience of the house to prolong the details of the advantages of Banks; especially since those, which might still be particularized are readily to be referred as consequences from those, which have been enumerated. Their disadvantages, real or supposed, are now to be reviewed. The most serious of the charges which have been brought against them are—

That they serve to increase usury:

That they tend to prevent other kinds of lending:

That they furnish temptations to overtrading:

That they afford aid to ignorant adventurers who disturb the natural and beneficial course of trade:

That they give to bankrupt and fraudulent traders a fictitious credit, which enables them to maintain false appearances and to extend their impositions: And lastly

That they have a tendency to banish gold and silver from the country.

There is great reason to believe, that on a close and candid survey, it will be discovered, that these charges are either destitute of foundation; or that, as far as the evils, they suggest, have been found to exist, they have proceeded from other, or partial, or temporary states, are not inherent in the nature and permanent tendency of such institutions; or are more than counterbalanced by opposite advantages. This survey shall be had, in the order in which the charges have been stated.

The first of them is, that Banks serve to increase usury.

It is a truth, which ought not to be denied, that the method of conducting business, which is essential to bank operations, has among us, in particular instances, given occasion to usurious transactions. The punctuality, in payments, which they necessarily exact has sometimes obliged those, who have adventured beyond both their capital and their credit to procure money, at any price, and consequently to resort to usurers for aid.

But experience and practice gradually bring a cure to this evil. A general habit of punctuality among traders is the natural consequence of the necessity of observing it with the Bank; a circumstance which itself more than compensates for any occasional ill, which may have sprung from that necessity, in the particular, under consideration. As far therefore as Traders depend on each other for pecuniary supplies, they can calculate their expectations with greater certainty; and are in proportionably less danger of disappointments, which might compel them to have recourse to so pernicious an expedient, as that of borrowing at usury; the mischiefs from which, after a few examples, naturally inspire great care, in all such men of desperate circumstances, to avoid the possibility of becoming subjected to them. One, and not the least of the evils incident to the use of that expedient, if the fact be known or even strongly suspected, is loss of credit with the bank itself.

The Directors of a bank too, though in order to extend its business and its popularity, in the infancy of an institution, they may be tempted to go further in accommodations, than the strict rules of prudence will warrant, grow more circumspect of course, as the affairs become better established, and as the evils of too great facility are experimentally demonstrated. They become more attentive to the situation and conduct of those, with whom they deal; they observe more narrowly their operations and pursuits; they economise the credit they give to those of suspicious solidity; they refuse it to those whose career is more manifestly hazardous. In a word, in the course of practice, from the very nature of things, their *interest* will make it the *policy* of a Bank, to succor the wary and industrious; to discredit the rash and unthrifty; to discountenance both usurious lenders and usurious borrowers.

There is a leading view, in which the tendency of banks will be seen to be, to abridge rather than to promote usury. This relates to their property of increasing the quantity and quickening the circulation of money. If it be evident, that usury will prevail or diminish according to the proportion which the demand for borrowing bears to the quantity of money at market to be lent; whatever has the property just mentioned, whether it be in the shape of paper or of coin, by contributing to render the supply more equal to the demand, must tend to counteract the progress of usury.

But bank-lending, it is pretended, is an impediment to other kinds of lending; which, by confining the resource of borrowing to a particular class, leaves the rest of the community more destitute, and therefore more exposed to the extortions of usurers. As the profits of bank stock exceed the legal rate of interest, the possessors of money, it is argued, prefer investing it in that article to lending it at this rate; to which there are the additional motives of a very prompt command of the capital, and of more frequent and exact returns, without trouble or perplexity in the collection. This constitutes the second charge, which has been enumerated.

The fact on which this charge rests is not to be admitted without several qualifications; particularly in reference to the state of things in this country. First. The great bulk of the Stock of a bank will consist of the funds of men in trade, among ourselves, and monied foreigners; the former of whom could not spare their capitals out of their reach, to be invested in loans, for long periods, on mortgages, or personal security; and the latter of whom would not be willing to be subjected to the casualties, delays and embarrassments of such a disposition of their money in a distant country. Secondly. There will always be a considerable proportion of those, who are properly the money lenders of a Country, who from that spirit of caution, which usually characterizes this description of men will incline rather to vest their funds in mortgages on real estate, than in the Stock of a Bank, which they are apt to consider as a more precarious security.

These considerations serve in a material degree to narrow the foundation of the objection, as to the point of fact. But there is a more satisfactory answer to it. The effect supposed, as far as it has existence, is temporary. The reverse of it takes place, in the general and permanent operation of the thing.

The capital of every public bank will of course be restricted within a certain defined limit. It is the province of legislative prudence so to adjust this limit, that while it will not be too contracted for the demand, which the course of business may create, and for the security, which the public ought to have for the solidity of the paper, which may be issued by the bank, it will still be within the compass of the pecuniary resources of the community; so that there may be an easy practicability of completing the subscriptions by it. When this is once done, the supposed effect of necessity ceases. There is then no longer room for the investment of any additional capital. Stock may indeed change hands by one person selling and another buying; but the money, which the buyer takes out of the common mass to purchase the stock, the seller receives, and restores to it. Hence the future surpluses, which may accumulate, must take their natural course, and lending at interest must go on, as if there were no such institution.

It must indeed flow in a more copious stream. The Bank furnishes an extraordinary supply for borrowers, within its immediate sphere. A larger supply consequently remains for borrowers elsewhere. In proportion, as the circulation of the Bank is extended, there is an augmentation of the aggregate mass of money, for answering the aggregate mass of demand. Hence a greater facility in obtaining it for every purpose.

It ought not to escape without a remark, that as far as the citizens of other countries become adventurers in the Bank, there is a positive increase of the gold and silver of the Country. It is true, that from this a half yearly rent is drawn back, accruing from the dividends upon the Stock. But as this rent arises from the employment of the capital, by our own citizens, it is probable, that it is more than replaced by the profits of that employment. It is also likely, that a part of it is, in the course of trade, converted into the products of our Country: And it may even prove an incentive, in some cases, to emigration to a country, in which the character of citizen is as easy to be acquired, as it is estimable and important. This view of the subject furnishes an answer to an objection, which has been deduced from the circumstance here taken notice of, namely the income resulting to foreigners from the part of the Stock, owned by them, which has been represented as tending to drain the country of its specie. In this objection, the original investment of the capital, and the constant use of it afterwards seem both to have been overlooked.

That Banks furnish temptations to overtrading is the third of the enumerated objections. This must mean, that by affording additional aids to mercantile enterprise, they induce the merchant sometimes to adventure beyond the prudent or salutary point. But the very statement of the thing shows, that the subject of the charge is an occasional ill, incident to a general good. Credit of every kind (as a species of which only can bank lending have the effect supposed) must be in different degrees, chargeable with the same inconvenience. It is even applicable to gold and silver, when they abound in circulation. But would it be wise on this account to decry the precious metals, to root out credit; or to proscribe the means of that enterprise, which is the main spring of trade and a principal source of national wealth, because it now and then runs into excesses, of which overtrading is one?

If the abuses of a beneficial thing are to determine its condemnation, there is scarcely a source of public prosperity, which will not speedily be closed. In every case, the evil is to be compared with the good; and in the present case such a comparison will issue in this, that the new and increased energies derived to commercial enterprise, from the aid of banks, are a source of general profit and advantage; which greatly outweigh the partial ills of the overtrading of a few individuals, at particular times, or of numbers of particular conjunctures.

The fourth and fifth charges may be considered together. These relate to the aid, which is sometimes afforded by banks to unskillful adventurers and fraudulent traders. These charges also have some degree of foundation; though far less than has been pretended, and they add to the instances of partial ills, connected with more extensive and overbalancing benefits.

The practice of giving fictitious credit to improper persons is one of those evils, which experience guided by interest speedily corrects. The bank itself is in so much jeopardy of being a sufferer by it, that it has the strongest of all inducements to be on its guard. It may not only be injured immediately by the delinquencies of the persons, to whom such credit is given; but eventually, by the incapacities of others, whom their impositions, or failures may have ruined.

Nor is there much danger of a bank's being betrayed into this error, from want of information. The Directors, themselves, being, for the most part, selected from the class of Traders are to be expected to possess individually an accurate knowledge of the characters and situations of those, who come within that description. And they have, in addition to this, the course of dealing of the persons themselves with the bank to assist their judgment, which is in most cases a good index of the state, in which those persons are. The artifices and shifts, which those in desperate or declining circumstances are obliged to employ, to keep up the countenance, which the rules of the Bank require, and the train of their connections, are so many prognostics, not difficult to be interpreted, of the fate which awaits them. Hence it not infrequently happens, that Banks are the first to discover the unsoundness of such characters, and, by withholding credit, to announce to the public, that they are not entitled to it.

If banks, in spite of every precaution, are sometimes betrayed into giving a false credit to the persons described; they more frequently enable honest and industrious men, of small or perhaps of no capital to undertake and prosecute business, with advantage to themselves and to the community; and assist merchants of both capital and credit, who meet with fortuitous and unforeseen shocks, which might without such helps prove fatal to them and to others; to make head against their misfortunes, and finally to retrieve their affairs: Circumstances, which form no inconsiderable encomium on the utility of Banks.

But the last and heaviest charge is still to be examined. This is, that Banks tend to banish the gold and silver of the Country.

The force of this objection rests upon their being an engine of paper credit, which by furnishing a substitute for the metals, is supposed to promote their exportation. It is an objection, which if it has any foundation, lies not against Banks, peculiarly, but against every species of paper credit.

The most common answer given to it is, that the thing supposed is of little, or no consequence; that it is immaterial what serves the purpose of money, whether paper or gold and silver; that the effect of both upon industry is the same; and that the intrinsic wealth of a nation is to be measured, not by the abundance of the precious metals, contained in it, but by the quantity of the productions of its labor and industry.

This answer is not destitute of solidity, though not entirely satisfactory. It is certain, that the vivification of industry, by a full circulation, with the aid of a proper and well regulated paper credit, may more than compensate for the loss of a part of the gold and silver of a Nation; if the consequence of avoiding that loss should be a scanty or defective circulation.

But the positive and permanent increase or decrease of the

precious metals, in a Country, can hardly ever be a matter of indifference. As the commodity taken in lieu of every other, it is a species of the most effective wealth; and as the money of the world, it is of great concern to the state, that it possess a sufficiency of it to face any demands, which the protection of its external interests may create.

The objection seems to admit of another and a more conclusive answer, which controverts the fact itself. A nation, that has no mines of its own, must derive the precious metals from others; generally speaking, in exchange for the products of its labor and industry. The quantity, it will possess, will therefore, in the ordinary course of things, be regulated by the favorable, or unfavorable balance of its trade; that is, by the proportion between its abilities to supply foreigners, and its wants of them; between the amount of its exportations and that of its importations. Hence the state of its agriculture and manufactures, the quantity and *quality* of its labor and industry must, in the main, influence and determine the increase or decrease of its gold and silver.

If this be true, the inference seems to be, that well constituted Banks favor the increase of the precious metals. It has been shown, that they augment in different ways, the active capital of the country. This, it is, which generates employment; which animates and expands labor and industry. Every addition, which is made to it, by contributing to put in motion a greater quantity of both, tends to create a greater quantity of the products of both: And, by furnishing more materials for exportation, conduces to a favorable balance of trade and consequently to the introduction and increase of gold and silver.

This conclusion appears to be drawn from solid premises. There are however objections to be made to it.

It may be said, that as Bank paper affords a substitute for specie, it serves to counteract that rigorous necessity for the metals, as a medium of circulation, which in the case of a wrong balance, might restrain in some degree their exportation; and it may be added, that from the same cause, in the same case, it would retard those economical and parsimonious reforms, in the manner of living, which the scarcity of money is calculated to produce, and which might be necessary to rectify such wrong balance.

There is perhaps some truth in both these observations; but they appear to be of a nature rather to form exceptions to the generality of the conclusion, than to overthrow it. The state of things, in which the *absolute exigencies* of circulation can be supposed to resist with any effect the urgent demands for specie, which a wrong balance of trade may occasion, presents an *extreme case*. And a situation in which a too expensive manner of living of a community, compared with its means, can stand in need of a corrective, from distress or necessity, is one, which perhaps rarely results, but from extraordinary and adventitious causes: such for example, as a national revolution, which unsettles all the established habits of a people, and inflames the appetite for extravagance, by the illusions of an ideal wealth, engendered by the continual multiplication of a depreciating currency or some similar cause. There is good reason to believe, that where the laws are wise and well executed, and the inviolability of property and contracts maintained, the economy of a people will, in the general course of things, correspond with its means.

The support of industry is probably in every case, of more consequence towards correcting a wrong balance of trade, than any practicable retrenchments, in the expenses of families, or individuals: And the stagnation of it would be likely to have more effect, in prolonging, than any such savings in shortening its continuance. That stagnation is a natural consequence of an inadequate medium, which, without the aid of Bank circulation, would in the cases supposed, be severely felt.

It also deserves notice, that as the circulation is always in a compound ratio to the fund, upon which it depends, and to the demand for it, and as that fund is itself affected by the exportation of the metals, there is no danger of its being overstocked, as in the case of paper issued at the pleasure of the Government; or of its preventing the consequences of any unfavorable balance from being sufficiently felt, to produce the reforms alluded to, as far as circumstances may require and admit.

Nothing can be more fallible, than the comparisons, which have been made between different countries, to illustrate the truth of the position under consideration. The comparative quantity of gold and silver, in different countries, depends upon an infinite variety of facts and combinations, all of which ought to be known, in order to judge, whether the existence or non existence of paper currencies has any share in the relative proportions they contain. The *mass* and *value* of the productions of the labor and industry of each, compared with its wants; the nature of its establishments abroad; the kind of wars in which it is usually engaged; the relations it bears to the countries, which are the original possessors of those metals; the privileges it enjoys in their trade; these and a number of other circumstances are all to be taken into the account, and render the investigation too complex to justify any reliance on the vague and general surmises, which have been hitherto hazarded on the point.

In the foregoing discussion, the objection has been considered as applying to the permanent expulsion and diminution of the metals. Their temporary exportation, for particular purposes, has not been contemplated. This, it must be confessed is facilitated by Banks, from the faculty they possess of supplying their place. But their utility is in nothing more conspicuous, than in these very cases. They enable the Government to pay its foreign debts, and to answer any exigencies, which the external concerns of the community may have produced. They enable the Merchant to support his credit, (on which the prosperity of trade depends) when special circumstances prevent remittances in other modes. They enable him also to prosecute enterprises, which ultimately tend to an augmentation of the species of wealth in question. It is evident, that gold and silver may often be employed in procuring commodities abroad; which, in a circuitous commerce, replace the original fund, with considerable addition. But it is not to be inferred from this facility given to temporary exportation, that

Banks, which are so friendly to trade and industry, are in their general tendency, inimical to the increase of the precious metals.

These several views of the subject appear sufficient to impress a full conviction, of the utility of Banks, and to demonstrate that they are of great importance, not only in relation to the administration of the finances, but in the general system of the political economy.

The judgment of many concerning them has no doubt been perplexed, by the misinterpretation of appearances, which were to be ascribed to other causes. The general devastation of personal property, occasioned by the late war, naturally produced, on the one hand, a great demand for money, and on the other a great deficiency of it to answer the demand. Some injudicious laws, which grew out of the public distresses, by impairing confidence and causing a part of the inadequate sum in the country to be locked up, aggravated the evil: The dissipated habits, contracted by many individuals, during the war, which after the peace plunged them into expenses beyond their incomes: The number of adventurers without capital and in many instances, without information, who at that epoch rushed into trade, and were obliged to make any sacrifices to support a transient credit; the employment of considerable sums in speculations upon the public debt, which from its unsettled state was incapable of becoming itself a substitute: All these circumstances concurring necessarily led to usurious borrowing, produced most of the inconveniences, and were the true causes of most of the appearances; which, where the Banks were established, have been by some erroneously placed to their account: a mistake, which they might easily have avoided, by turning their eyes towards places, where there were none, and where, nevertheless, the same evils would have been perceived to exist, even in a greater degree, than where those institutions had obtained.

These evils have either ceased, or been greatly mitigated. Their more complete extinction may be looked for, from that additional security to property, which the constitution of the

United States happily gives (a circumstance of prodigious moment in the scale both of public and private prosperity) from the attraction of foreign capital, under the auspices of that security, to be employed upon objects and in enterprises, for which the state of this country opens a wide and inviting field, from the consistency and stability, which the public debt is fast acquiring, as well in the public opinion, at home and abroad, as in fact; from the augmentation of capital, which that circumstance and the quarter yearly payment of interest will afford; and from the more copious circulation, which will be likely to be created by a well constituted National Bank.

The establishment of Banks in this country seems to be recommended by reasons of a peculiar nature. Previously to the revolution circulation was in a great measure carried on by paper emitted by the several local governments. In Pennsylvania alone the quantity of it was near a million and a half of dollars. This auxiliary may be said to be now at an end. And it is generally supposed, that there has been for some time past, a deficiency of circulating medium. How far that deficiency is to be considered as real or imaginary is not susceptible of demonstration, but there are circumstances and appearances, which, in relation to the country at large, countenance the supposition of its reality.

The circumstances are, besides the fact just mentioned respecting paper emissions the vast tracts of waste land, and the little advanced state of manufactures. The progressive settlement of the former, while it promises ample retribution, in the generation of future resources, diminishes or obstructs, in the mean time, the active wealth of the country. It not only draws off a part of the circulating money, and places it in a more passive state, but it diverts into its own channels a portion of that species of labor and industry, which would otherwise be employed, in furnishing materials for foreign trade, and which by contributing to a favorable balance, would assist the introduction of specie. In the early periods of new settlements, the settlers not only furnish no surplus for exportation, but they consume a part of that which is produced by the labor of others. The same thing is a cause, that manufactures do not advance or advance slowly. And notwithstanding some hypotheses to the contrary, there are many things to induce a suspicion, that the precious metals will not abound, in any country, which has not mines or variety of manufactures. They have been sometimes acquired by the sword, but the modern system of war has expelled this resource, and it is one upon which it is to be hoped the United States will never be inclined to rely.

The appearances, alluded to, are, greater prevalence of direct barter, in the more interior districts of the country, which however has been for some time past gradually lessening; and greater difficulty, generally, in the advantageous alienation of improved real estate; which, also, has, of late, diminished, but is still seriously felt in different parts of the Union. The difficulty of getting money, which has been a general complaint, is not added to the number; because it is the complaint of all times, and one, in which imagination must ever have too great scope, to permit an appeal to it.

If the supposition of such a deficiency be in any degree founded, and some aid to circulation be desirable, it remains to inquire what ought to be the nature of that aid.

The emitting of paper money by the authority of Government is wisely prohibited to the individual States, by the National Constitution. And the spirit of that prohibition ought not to be disregarded, by the Government of the United States. Though paper emissions, under a general authority, might have some advantages, not applicable, and be free from some disadvantages, which are applicable, to the like emissions by the states separately; yet they are of a nature so liable to abuse, and it may even be affirmed so certain of being abused, that the wisdom of the Government will be shown in never trusting itself with the use of so seducing and dangerous an expedient. In times of tranquility, it might have no ill consequence, it might even perhaps be managed in a way to be productive of good; but in great and trying emergencies, there is almost a moral certainty of its becoming mischievous. The stamping of paper is an operation so much easier than the laying of taxes, that a government, in the practice of paper emissions, would rarely fail in any such emergency to indulge itself too far, in the employment of that resource, to avoid as much as possible one less auspicious to present popularity. If it should not even be carried so far as to be rendered an absolute bubble, it would at least be likely to be extended to a degree, which would occasion an inflated and artificial state of things incompatible with the regular and prosperous course of the political economy.

Among other material differences between a paper currency, issued by the mere authority of Government, and one issued by a Bank, payable in coin, is this—That in the first case, there is no standard to which an appeal can be made, as to the quantity which will only satisfy, or which will surcharge the circulation; in the last, that standard results from the demand. If more should be issued, than is necessary, it will return upon the bank. Its emissions, as elsewhere intimated, must always be in a compound ratio to the fund and to the demand: Whence it is evident, that there is a limitation in the nature of the thing: While the discretion of the government is the only measure of the extent of the emissions, by its own authority.

This consideration further illustrates the danger of emissions of that sort, and the preference, which is due to Bank paper.

The payment of the interest of the public debt, at thirteen different places, is a weighty reason, peculiar to our immediate situation, for desiring a Bank circulation. Without a paper, in general currency, equivalent to gold and silver, a considerable proportion of the specie of the country must always be suspended from circulation and left to accumulate, preparatorily to each day of payment; and as often as one approaches, there must in several cases be an actual transportation of the metals at both expense and risk, from their natural and proper reservoirs to distant places. This necessity will be felt very injuriously to the trade of some of the States; and will embarrass not a little the operations of the Treasury in those States. It will also obstruct those negotiations, between different parts of the Union, by the instrumentality of Treasury bills, which have already afforded valuable accommodations to Trade in general.

Assuming it then as a consequence, from what has been said, that a national bank is a desirable institution; two inquiries emerge. Is there no such institution, already in being, which has a claim to that character, and which supersedes the propriety, or necessity of another? If there be none, what are the principles upon which one ought to be established?

There are at present three banks in the United States. That of North America, established in the city of Philadelphia; that of New York, established in the city of New York; that of Massachusetts, established in the city of Boston. Of these three, the first is the only one, which has at any time had a direct relation to the Government of the United States.

The Bank of North America originated in a resolution of Congress of the 26th of May 1781, founded upon a proposition of the Superintendant of finance, which was afterwards carried into execution, by an ordinance of the 31st of December following, entitled, "An Ordinance to incorporate the Subscribers to the Bank of North America."

The aid afforded to the United States, by this institution, during the remaining period of the war, was of essential consequence, and its conduct towards them since the peace, has not weakened its title to their patronage and favor. So far its pretensions to the character in question are respectable; but there are circumstances, which militate against them; and considerations, which indicate the propriety of an establishment on different principles.

The Directors of this Bank, on behalf of their constituents, have since *accepted* and *acted* under a new charter from the State of Pennsylvania, materially variant from their original one; and which so narrows the foundation of the institution, as to render it an incompetent basis for the extensive purposes of a National Bank.

The limit assigned by the ordinance of Congress to the Stock of the Bank is ten millions of Dollars. The last charter of Pennsylvania confines it to two millions. Questions naturally arise, whether there be not a direct repugnancy between two charters so differently circumstanced; and whether the acceptance of the one is not to be deemed a virtual surrender of the other. But perhaps it is neither advisable nor necessary to attempt a solution of them.

There is nothing in the Acts of Congress, which imply an exclusive right in the institution, to which they relate, except during the term of the war. There is therefore nothing, if the public good require it, which prevents the establishment of another. It may however be incidentally remarked, that in the general opinion of the citizens of the United States, the Bank of North America has taken the station of a bank of Pennsylvania only. This is a strong argument for a new institution, or for a renovation of the old, to restore it to the situation in which it originally stood, in the view of the United States.

But though the ordinance of Congress contains no grant of exclusive privileges, there may be room to allege, that the Government of the United States ought not, in point of candor and equity, to establish any rival or interfering institution, in prejudice of the one already established; especially as this has, from services rendered, well founded claims to protection and regard.

The justice of such an observation ought within proper bounds to be admitted. A new establishment of the sort ought not to be made, without cogent and sincere reasons of public good. And in the manner of doing it every facility should be given to a consolidation of the old with the new, upon terms not injurious to the parties concerned. But there is no ground to maintain, that in a case, in which the Government has made no condition restricting its authority, it ought voluntarily to restrict it, through regard to the interests of a particular institution, when those of the state dictate a different course; especially too after such circumstances have intervened, as characterize the actual situation of the Bank of North America.

The inducements, to a new disposition of the thing are now to be considered. The first of them which occurs is, the, at least ambiguous, situation, in which the Bank of North America has placed itself, by the acceptance of its last charter. If this has rendered it the mere Bank of a particular state, liable to dissolution at the expiration of fourteen years, to which term the act of that state has restricted its duration, it would be neither fit nor expedient to accept it, as an equivalent for a Bank of the United States.

The restriction of its capital also, which according to the same supposition, cannot be extended beyond two millions of dollars, is a conclusive reason for a different establishment. So small a capital promises neither the requisite aid to government, nor the requisite security to the community. It may answer very well the purposes of local accommodation, but is an inadequate foundation for a circulation coextensive with the United States, embracing the whole of their revenues, and affecting every individual, into whose hands the paper may come.

And inadequate as such a capital would be to the essential ends of a National Bank, it is liable to being rendered still more so, by that principle of the constitution of the Bank of North America, contained equally in its old and in its new charter, which leaves the increase of the *actual* capital at any time (now far short of the allowed extent) to the discretion of the Directors, or Stockholders. It is naturally to be expected, that the allurements of an advanced price of Stock and or large dividends may disincline those, who are interested, to an extension of capital; from which they will be apt to fear a diminution of profits. And from this circumstance, the interest and accommodation of the public (as well individually as collectively) are made more subordinate to the interest, real or imagined, of the Stockholders, than they ought to be. It is true, that unless the latter be consulted, there can be no bank (in the sense at least in which institutions of this kind, worthy of confidence, can be established in this Country) but it does not follow, that this is alone to be consulted, or that it even ought to be paramount. Public utility is more truly the object of public Banks, than private profit. And it is the business of Government, to constitute them on such principles, that while the latter will result, in a sufficient degree, to afford competent motives to engage in them, the former be not made subservient to it. To effect this, a principal object of attention ought to be to give free scope to the creation of an ample capital; and with this view, fixing the bounds, which are deemed safe and convenient, to leave no discretion either to stop short of them or to overpass them. The want of this precaution, in the establishment of the Bank of North America, is a further and an important reason for desiring one differently constituted.

There may be room, at first sight, for a supposition, that as the profits of a Bank will bear a proportion to the extent of its operations, and as, for this reason, the interest of the Stockholders will not be disadvantageously affected, by any necessary augmentations of capital, there is no cause to apprehend, that they will be indisposed to such augmentations. But most men in matters of this nature, prefer the certainties, they enjoy, to probabilities depending on untried experiments; especially when these promise rather, that they will not be injured, than that they will be benefited.

From the influence of this principle, and a desire of enhancing its profits, the Directors of a Bank will be more apt to overstrain its faculties, in the attempt to face the additional demands, which the course of business may create, than to set on foot new subscriptions, which may hazard a diminution of the profits, and even a temporary reduction of the price of Stock.

Banks are among the best expedients for lowering the rate of interest, in a country; but to have this effect, their capitals must be completely equal to all the demands of business, and such as will tend to remove the idea, that the accommodations they afford, are in any degree favors; an idea very apt to accompany the parsimonious dispensation of contracted funds. In this, as in every other case, the plenty of the commodity ought to beget a moderation of the price.

The want of a principle of rotation, in the constitution of the Bank of North America, is another argument for a variation of the establishment. Scarcely one of the reasons, which militate against this principle in the constitution of a country, is applicable to that of a Bank; while there are strong reasons in favor of it, in relation to the one, which do not apply to the other. The knowledge, to be derived from experience, is the only circumstance common to both, which pleads against rotation in the directing officers of a Bank.

But the objects of the Government of a nation, and those of the government of a bank are so widely different, as greatly to weaken the force of that consideration, in reference to the latter. Almost every important case of legislation requires, towards a right decision, a general and an accurate acquaintance with the affairs of the state; and habits of thinking seldom acquired, but from a familiarity with public concerns. The administration of a bank, on the contrary, is regulated, by a few simple fixed maxims, the application of which is not difficult to any man of judgment, especially if instructed in the principles of trade. It is in general a constant succession of the same details.

But though this be the case, the idea of the advantages of experience is not to be slighted. Room ought to be left for the regular transmission of official information: And for this purpose the head of the direction ought to be excepted from the principle of rotation. With this exception, and with the aid of the information of the subordinate officers, there can be no danger of any ill effects from want of experience, or knowledge; especially as the periodical exclusion ought not to reach the whole of the Directors at one time; The argument in favor of the principle of rotation is this, that by lessening the danger of combinations among the Directors, to make the institution subservient to party views, or to the accommodation, preferably, of any particular set of men, it will render the public confidence more firm, stable and unqualified.

When it is considered, that the Directors of a Bank are not elected by the great body of the community, in which a diversity of views will naturally prevail, at different conjunctures, but by a small and select class of men, among whom it is far more easy to cultivate a steady adherence to the same persons and objects; and that those Directors have it in their power so immediately to conciliate, by obliging the most influential of this class, it is easy to perceive, that without the principle of rotation, changes in that body can rarely happen, but as a concession which they may themselves think it expedient to make to public opinion.

The continual administration of an institution of this kind, by the same persons, will never fail, with, or without, cause, from their conduct, to excite distrust and discontent. The necessary secrecy of their transactions gives unlimited scope to imagination to infer that something is, or may be wrong. And this inevitable mystery is a solid reason, for inserting in the constitution of a Bank the necessity of a change of men. As neither the mass of the parties interested nor the public in general can be permitted to be witnesses of the interior management of the Directors, it is reasonable, that both should have that check upon their conduct, and that security against the prevalency of a partial or pernicious system, which will be produced by the certainty of periodical changes. Such too is the delicacy of the credit of a Bank, that every thing, which can fortify confidence and repel suspicion, without injuring its operations, ought carefully to be sought after in its formation.

A further consideration in favor of a change, is the improper rule, by which the right of voting for Directors is regulated in the plan, upon which the Bank of North America was originally constituted, namely a vote for each share, and the want of a rule in the last charter; unless the silence of it, on that point, may signify that every Stockholder is to have an equal and a single vote, which would be a rule in a different extreme not less erroneous. It is of importance that a rule should be established, on this head, as it is one of those things, which ought not to be left to discretion;

and it is consequently, of equal importance, that the rule should be a proper one.

A vote for each share renders a combination, between a few principal Stockholders, to monopolize the power and benefits of the Bank too easy. An equal vote to each Stockholder, however great or small his interest in the institution, allows not that degree of weight to large stockholders, which it is reasonable they should have, and which perhaps their security and that of the bank require. A prudent mean is to be preferred. A conviction of this has produced a by-law of the corporation of the bank of North America, which evidently aims at such a mean. But a reflection arises here, that a like majority with that which enacted this law, may at any moment repeal it.

The last inducement, which shall be mentioned, is the want of precautions to guard against a foreign influence insinuating itself into the Direction of the Bank. It seems scarcely reconcilable with a due caution to permit, that any but citizens should be eligible as Directors of a National Bank, or that non-resident foreigners should be able to influence the appointment of Directors by the votes of their proxies. In the event however of an incorporation of the Bank of North America in the plan, it may be necessary to qualify this principle, so as to leave the right of foreigners, who now hold shares of its stock unimpaired; but without the power of transmitting the privilege in question to foreign alienees.

It is to be considered, that such a Bank is not a mere matter of private property, but a political machine of the greatest importance to the State.

There are other variations from the Constitution of the Bank of North America, not of inconsiderable moment, which appear desirable, but which are not of magnitude enough to claim a preliminary discussion. These will be seen in the plan, which will be submitted in the sequel.

If the objections, which have been stated to the constitution of the Bank of North America, are admitted to be well founded, they will nevertheless not derogate from the merit of the main design, or of the services which that bank has rendered, or of the benefits which it has produced. The creation of such an institution, at the time it took place, was a measure dictated by wisdom. Its utility has been amply evinced by its fruits. American Independence owes much to it. And it [is] very conceivable, that reasons of the moment may have rendered those features in it inexpedient which a revision, with a permanent view, suggests as desirable.

The order of the subject leads next to an inquiry into the principles, upon which a national Bank, ought to be organized.

The situation of the United States naturally inspires a wish, that the form of the institution could admit of a plurality of branches. But various considerations discourage from pursuing this idea. The complexity of such a plan would be apt to inspire doubts, which might deter from adventuring in it. And the practicability of a safe and orderly administration, though not to be abandoned as desperate cannot be made so manifest in perspective, as to promise the removal of those doubts, or to justify the Government in adopting the idea as an original experiment. The most that would seem advisable, on this point, is to insert a provision, which may lead to it hereafter; if experience shall more clearly demonstrate its utility, and satisfy those, who may have the Direction, that it may be adopted with safety. It is certain, that it would have some advantages both peculiar and important. Besides more general accommodation, it would lessen the danger of a run upon the bank.

The argument, against it, is, that each branch must be under a distinct, though subordinate direction; to which a considerable latitude of discretion must of necessity be entrusted. And as the property of the whole institution would be liable for the engagements of each part, that and its credit would be at stake, upon the prudence of the Directors of every part. The mismanagement of either branch, might hazard serious disorder in the whole.

Another wish, dictated by the particular situation of the

country, is, that the Bank could be so constituted as to be made an immediate instrument of loans to the proprietors of land; but this wish also yields to the difficulty of accomplishing it. Land is alone an unfit fund for a bank circulation. If the notes issued upon it were not to be payable in coin, on demand, or at a short date; this would amount to nothing more than a repetition of the paper emissions, which are now exploded by the general voice. If the notes are to be payable in coin, the land must first be converted into it by sale, or mortgage. The difficulty of effecting the latter is the very thing, which begets the desire of finding another resource, and the former would not be practicable on a sudden emergency, but with sacrifices which would make the cure worse than the disease. Neither is the idea of constituting the fund partly of coin and partly of land free from impediments. These two species of property do not for the most part unite in the same hands. Will the monied man consent to enter into a partnership with the landholder by which the *latter* will share in the profits which will be made by the money of the *former?* The money it is evident will be the agent or efficient cause of the profits. The land can only be regarded as an additional security. It is not difficult to foresee, that an union, on such terms, will not readily be formed. If the landholders are to procure the money by sale or mortgage of a part of their lands, this they can as well do, when the Stock consists wholly of money, as if it were to be compounded of money and land.

To procure for the landholders the assistance of loans is the great desideratum. Supposing other difficulties surmounted, and a fund created, composed partly of coin and partly of land, yet the benefit contemplated could only then be obtained, by the banks advancing them its notes for the whole or part of the value of the lands, they had subscribed to the Stock. If this advance was small, the relief aimed at would not be given; if it was large, the quantity of notes issued would be a cause of *distrust*, and, if received at all, they would be likely to return speedily upon the Bank for payment; which, after exhausting its coin, might be under a necessity of turning its lands into money, at any price, that could be obtained for them, to the irreparable prejudice of the proprietors.

Considerations of public advantage suggest a further wish, which is, that the Bank could be established upon principles, that would cause the profits of it to redound to the immediate benefit of the State. This is contemplated by many, who speak of a National Bank, but the idea seems liable to insuperable objections. To attach full confidence to an institution of this nature, it appears to be an essential ingredient in its structure, that it shall be under a private not a public Direction, under the guidance of individual interest, not of public policy; which would be supposed to be, and in certain emergencies, under a feeble or too sanguine administration would, really, be, liable to being too much influenced by public necessity. The suspicion of this would most probably be a canker, that would continually corrode the vitals of the credit of the Bank, and would be most likely to prove fatal in those situations; in which the public good would require, that they should be most sound and vigorous. It would indeed be little less, than a miracle, should the credit of the Bank be at the disposal of the Government, if in a long series of time, there was not experienced a calamitous abuse of it. It is true, that it would be the real interest of the Government not to abuse it; its genuine policy to husband and cherish it with the most guarded circumspection as an inestimable treasure. But what Government ever uniformly consulted its true interest, in opposition to the temptations of momentary exigencies? What nation was ever blessed with a constant succession of upright and wise Administrators?

The keen, steady, and, as it were, magnetic sense, of their own interest, as proprietors, in the Directors of a Bank, pointing invariably to its true pole, the prosperity of the institution, is the only security, that can always be relied upon, for a careful and prudent administration. It is therefore the only basis on which an enlightened, unqualified and permanent confidence can be expected to be erected and maintained.

The precedents of the Banks established in several cities of Europe, Amsterdam, Hamburg and others, may seem to militate against this position. Without a precise knowledge of all the peculiarities of their respective constitutions, it is difficult to pronounce how far this may be the case. That of Amsterdam, however, which we best know, is rather under a municipal than a governmental direction. Particular magistrates of the city, not officers of the republic, have the management of it. It is also a Bank of deposit, not of loan, or circulation; consequently less liable to abuse, as well as less useful. Its general business consists in receiving money for safekeeping; which if not called for within a certain time becomes a part of its Stock and irreclaimable: But a Credit is given for it on the books of the Bank, which being transferable, answers all the purposes of money.

The Directors being Magistrates of the city, and the Stockholders in general, its most influential citizens, it is evident, that the principle of private interest must be prevalent in the management of the Bank. And it is equally evident, that from the nature of its operations, that principle is less essential to it, than to an Institution constituted with a view to the accommodation of the Public and Individuals by direct loans and a paper circulation.

As far as may concern the aid of the Bank, within the proper limits, a good government has nothing more to wish for, than it will always possess; though the management be in the hands of private individuals. As the institution, if rightly constituted, must depend for its renovation from time to time on the pleasure of the Government, it will not be likely to feel a disposition to render itself, by its conduct, unworthy of public patronage. The Government too in the administration of its finances, has it in its power to reciprocate benefits to the Bank, of not less importance, than those which the bank affords to the Government, and which besides are never unattended with an immediate and adequate compensation. Independent of these more particular considerations, the natural weight and influence of a good Government will always go far towards procuring a compliance with its desires; and as the Directors will usually be composed of some of the most discreet, respectable and well informed citizens, it can hardly ever be difficult to make them sensible of the force of the inducements, which ought to stimulate their exertions.

It will not follow, from what has been said, that the state may not be the holder of a part of the Stock of a Bank, and consequently a sharer in the profits of it. It will only follow, that it ought not to desire any participation in the Direction of it, and therefore ought not to own the whole or a principal part of the Stock; for if the mass of the property should belong to the public, and if the direction of it should be in private hands, this would be to commit the interests of the state to persons, not interested, or not enough interested in their proper management.

There is one thing, however, which the Government owes to itself and to the community; at least to all that part of it, who are not Stockholders; which is to reserve to itself a right of ascertaining, as often as may be necessary, the state of the Bank, excluding however all pretension to control. This right forms an article in the primitive constitution of the Bank of North America. And its propriety stands upon the clearest reasons. If the paper of a Bank is to be permitted to insinuate itself into all the revenues and receipts of a country; if it is even to be tolerated as the substitute for gold and silver, in all the transactions of business, it becomes in either view a national concern of the first magnitude. As such the ordinary rules of prudence require, that the Government should possess the means of ascertaining, whenever it thinks fit, that so delicate a trust is executed with fidelity and care. A right of this nature is not only desirable, as it respects the Government; but it ought to be equally so to all those, concerned in the institution; as an additional title to public and private confidence; and as a thing which can only be formidable to practices, that imply mismanagement. The presumption must always be, that the characters who would be entrusted with the exercise of this right, on behalf of the Government, will not be deficient in the discretion, which it may require; at least the admitting of this presumption cannot be deemed too great a return of confidence for that very large portion of it, which the Government is required to place in the Bank.

Abandoning, therefore, ideas, which however agreeable or desirable, are neither practicable nor safe, the following plan for the constitution of a National Bank is respectfully submitted to the consideration of the House.

I. The capital Stock of the Bank shall not exceed ten Millions of Dollars, divided into Twenty five thousand shares, each share being four hundred Dollars; to raise which sum, subscriptions shall be opened on the first Monday of April next, and shall continue open, until the whole shall be subscribed. Bodies politic as well as individuals may subscribe.

II. The amount of each share shall be payable, one fourth in gold and silver coin, and three fourths in that part of the public debt, which according to the loan proposed by the Act making provision for the debt of the United States, shall bear an accruing interest at the time of payment of six percent per annum.

III. The respective sums subscribed shall be payable in four equal parts, as well specie as debt, in succession, and at the distance of six calendar months from each other; the first payment to be made at the time of subscription. If there shall be a failure in any subsequent payment, the party failing shall lose the benefit of any dividend which may have accrued, prior to the time for making such payment, and during the delay of the same.

IV. The Subscribers to the Bank and their successors shall be incorporated, and shall so continue until the final redemption of that part of its stock, which shall consist of the public debt.

V. The capacity of the corporation to hold real and personal estate shall be limited to fifteen millions of Dollars, including the amount of its capital, or original stock. The lands and tenements, which it shall be permitted to hold, shall be only such as shall be requisite for the immediate accommodation of the institution; and such as shall have been bona fide mortgaged to it by way of security, or conveyed to it in satisfaction of debts previously contracted, in the usual course of its dealings, or purchased at sales upon judgments which shall have been obtained for such debts.

VI. The totality of the debts of the company, whether by bond, bill, note, or other contract, (credits for deposits excepted) shall never exceed the amount of its capital stock. In case of excess, the Directors, under whose administration it shall happen, shall be liable for it in their private or separate capacities. Those who may have dissented may excuse themselves from this responsibility by immediately giving notice of the fact and their dissent to the President of the United States, and to the Stockholders, at a general meeting to be called by the President of the Bank at their request.

VII. The Company may sell or demise its lands and tenements, or may sell the whole, or any part of the public Debt, whereof its Stock shall consist; but shall trade in nothing, except bills of exchange, gold and silver bullion, or in the sale of goods pledged for money lent: nor shall take more than at the rate of six percent, per annum, upon its loans or discounts.

VIII. No loan shall be made by the bank, for the use or on account of the Government of the United States, or of either of them to an amount exceeding fifty thousand Dollars, or of any foreign prince or State; unless previously authorised by a law of the United States.

IX. The Stock of the Bank shall be transferable according to such rules as shall be instituted by the Company in that behalf.

X. The affairs of the Bank shall be under the management of Twenty five Directors, one of whom shall be the President. And there shall be on the first Monday of January, in each year, a choice of Directors, by plurality of suffrages of the Stockholders, to serve for a year. The Directors at their first meeting, after each election, shall choose one of their number as President.

XI. The number of votes, to which each Stockholder shall be entitled, shall be according to the number of shares he shall hold in the proportions following, that is to say, for one share and not more than two shares one vote; for every two shares, above two and, not exceeding ten, one vote; for every four shares above ten and not exceeding thirty, one vote; for every six shares above thirty and not exceeding sixty, one vote; for every eight shares above sixty and not exceeding one hundred, one vote; and for every ten shares above one hundred, one vote; but no person, copartnership, or body politic, shall be entitled to a greater number than thirty votes. And after the first election, no share or shares shall confer a right of suffrage, which shall not have been held three calendar months previous to the day of election. Stockholders actually resident within the United States and none other may vote in elections by proxy.

XII. Not more than three fourths of the Directors in office, exclusive of the President, shall be eligible for the next succeeding year. But the Director who shall be President at the time of an election may always be reelected.

XIII. None but a Stockholder being a citizen of the United States, shall be eligible as a Director.

XIV. Any number of Stockholders not less than sixty, who together shall be proprietors of two hundred shares, or upwards, shall have power at any time to call a general meeting of the Stockholders, for purposes relative to the Institution; giving at least six weeks notice in two public gazettes of the place where the Bank is kept and specifying in such notice the object of the meeting.

XV. In case of the death, resignation, absence from the United States, or removal of a Director by the Stockholders, his place may be filled by a new choice for the remainder of the year.

XVI. No Director shall be entitled to any emolument, unless the same shall have been allowed by the Stockholders at a General meeting. The Stockholders shall make such compensation to the President, for his extraordinary attendance at the Bank, as shall appear to them reasonable.

XVII. Not less than seven Directors shall constitute a Board for the transaction of business.

XVIII. Every Cashier, or Treasurer, before he enters on the

duties of his office shall be required to give bond, with two or more sureties, to the satisfaction of the Directors, in a sum not less than twenty thousand Dollars, with condition for his good behavior.

XIX. Half yearly dividends shall be made of so much of the profits of the Bank as shall appear to the Directors advisable: And once in every three years the Directors shall lay before the Stockholders, at a General Meeting, for their information, an exact and particular statement of the debts, which shall have remained unpaid, after the expiration of the original credit, for a period of treble the term of that credit; and of the surplus of profit, if any, after deducting losses and dividends.

XX. The bills and notes of the Bank originally made payable, or which shall have become payable on demand, in gold and silver coin, shall be receivable in all payments to the United States.

XXI. The Officer at the head of the Treasury Department of the United States, shall be furnished from time to time, as often as he may require, not exceeding once a week, with statements of the amount of the capital Stock of the Bank and of the debts due to the same; of the monies deposited therein; of the notes in circulation, and of the Cash in hand; and shall have a right to inspect such general account in the books of the bank as shall relate to the said statements; provided, that this shall not be construed to imply a right of inspecting this account of any private individual or individuals with the Bank.

XXII. No similar institution shall be established by any future act of the United States, during the continuance of the one hereby proposed to be established.

XXIII. It shall be lawful for the Directors of the Bank to establish offices, wheresoever they shall think fit, within the United States, for the purposes of discount and deposit only, and upon the same terms, and in the same manner, as shall be practiced at the Bank; and to commit the management of the said offices, and the making of the said discounts, either to Agents specially appointed by them, or to such persons as may be chosen by the

Stockholders residing at the place where any such office shall be, under such agreements and subject to such regulations as they shall deem proper; not being contrary to law or to the Constitution of the Bank.

XXIV. And lastly. The President of the United States shall be authorised to cause a subscription to be made to the Stock of the said Company, on behalf of the United States, to an amount not exceeding two Millions of Dollars, to be paid out of the monies which shall be borrowed by virtue of either of the Acts, the one entitled "an Act making provision for the debt of the United States," and the other entitled "An Act making provision for the reduction of the Public Debt"; borrowing of the bank an equal sum, to be applied to the purposes for which the said monies shall have been procured, reimbursable in ten years by equal annual installments; or at any time sooner, or in any greater proportions, that the Government may think fit.

The reasons for the several provisions contained in the foregoing plan, have been so far anticipated, and will, for the most part, be so readily suggested, by the nature of those provisions, that any comments, which need further be made, will be both few and concise.

The combination of a portion of the public Debt in the formation of the Capital, is the principal thing, of which an explanation is requisite. The chief object of this is, to enable the creation of a capital sufficiently large to be the basis of an extensive circulation, and an adequate security for it. As has been elsewhere remarked, the original plan of the Bank of North America contemplated a capital of ten millions of Dollars, which is certainly not too broad a foundation for the extensive operations, to which a National Bank is destined. But to collect such a sum in this country, in gold and silver into one depository, may, without hesitation, be pronounced impracticable. Hence the necessity of an auxiliary which the public debt at once presents.

This part of the fund will be always ready to come in aid of the specie. It will more and more command a ready sale; and can therefore expeditiously be turned into coin if an exigency of the Bank should at any time require it. This quality of prompt convertibility into coin, renders it an equivalent for that necessary agent of Bank circulation; and distinguished it from a fund in land of which the sale would generally be far less compendious and at great disadvantage. The quarter yearly receipts of interest will also be an actual addition to the specie fund during the intervals between them and the half yearly dividends of profits. The objection to combining land with specie, resulting from their not being generally in possession of the same persons, does not apply to the debt which will always be found in considerable quantity among the monied and trading people.

The debt composing part of the capital, besides its collateral effect in enabling the Bank to extend its operations, and consequently to enlarge its profits, will produce a direct annual revenue of six percent from the Government, which will enter into the half yearly dividends received by the Stockholders.

When the present price of the public debt is considered, and the effect which its conversion into Bank Stock, incorporated with a specie fund, would in all probability have to accelerate its rise to the proper point, it will easily be discovered, that the operation presents in its outset a very considerable advantage to those who may become subscribers; and from the influence, which that rise would have on the general mass of the Debt, a proportional benefit to all the public creditors, and, in a sense, which has been more than once adverted to, to the community at large.

There is an important fact, which exemplifies the fitness of the public Debt, for a bank fund, and which may serve to remove doubts in some minds on this point. It is this, that the Bank of England in its first erection rested wholly on that foundation. The subscribers to a Loan to Government of one million two hundred thousand pounds sterling were incorporated as a Bank; of which the Debt created by the Loan, and the interest upon it, were the sole fund. The subsequent augmentations of its capital, which now amounts to between eleven and twelve millions of pounds sterling, have been of the same nature.

The confining of the right of the Bank to contract debts to the amount of its capital is an important precaution, which is not to be found in the constitution of the Bank of North America, and which, while the fund consists wholly of coin, would be a restriction attended with inconveniencies, but would be free from any if the composition of it should be such as is now proposed. The restriction exists in the establishment of the Bank of England, and as a source of security is worthy of imitation. The consequence of exceeding the limit there is, that each Stockholder is liable to the excess, in proportion to his interest in the Bank. When it is considered, that the Directors owe their appointments to the choice of the Stockholders, a responsibility of this kind, on the part of the latter, does not appear unreasonable. But, on the other hand, it may be deemed a hardship upon those, who may have dissented from the choice. And there are many among us, whom it might perhaps discourage from becoming concerned in the institution. These reasons have induced the placing of the responsibility upon the Directors, by whom the limit prescribed should be transgressed.

The interdiction of loans on account of the United States, or of any particular state, beyond the moderate sum specified, or of any foreign power, will serve as a barrier to executive encroachments; and to combinations inauspicious to the safety or contrary to the policy of the Union.

The limitation of the rate of interest is dictated by the consideration, that different rates prevail in different parts of the Union; and as the operations of the Bank may extend through the whole, some rule seems to be necessary. There is room for a question, whether the limitation ought not rather to be to five than to six percent, as proposed. It may with safety be taken for granted, that the former rate would yield an ample dividend; perhaps as much as the latter, by the extension which it would give to business. The natural effect of low interest is to increase trade and industry; because undertakings of every kind can be prosecuted with greater advantage. This is a truth generally admitted; but it is requisite to have analyzed the subject, in all its relations, to be able to form a just conception of the extent of that effect. Such an analysis cannot but satisfy an intelligent mind, that the difference of one percent, in the rate at which money may be had, is often capable of making an essential change for the better in the situation of any country or place.

Every thing, therefore, which tends to lower the rate of interest is peculiarly worthy of the cares of Legislators. And though laws which violently sink the legal rate of interest greatly below the market level are not to be commended, because they are not calculated to answer their aim, yet whatever has a tendency to effect a reduction, without violence to the natural course of things, ought to be attended to and pursued. Banks are among the means most proper to accomplish this end; and the moderation of the rate at which their discounts are made, is a material ingredient towards it; with which their own interest, viewed on an enlarged and permanent scale, does not appear to clash.

But as the most obvious ideas are apt to have greater force, than those which depend on complex and remote combinations, there would be danger, that the persons whose funds must constitute the Stock of the Bank would be diffident of the sufficiency of the profits to be expected, if the rate of loans and discounts were to be placed below the point to which they have been accustomed; and might on this account be indisposed to embarking in the plan. There is, it is true, one reflection, which in regard to men actively engaged in trade ought to be a security against this danger; it is this, that the accommodations which they might derive in the way of their business, at a low rate, would more than indemnify them for any difference in the dividend, supposing even that some diminution of it were to be the consequence. But upon the whole, the hazard of contrary reasoning among the mass of monied men is a powerful argument against the experiment. The institutions of the kind already existing add to the difficulty of making it. Maturer reflection and a large capital may of themselves lead to the desired end.

The last thing, which will require any explanatory remark, is the authority proposed to be given to the President to subscribe to the amount of two millions of Dollars on account of the public. The main design of this is to enlarge the specie fund of the Bank, and to enable it to give a more early extension to its operations. Though it is proposed to borrow with one hand what is lent with the other, yet the disbursement of what is borrowed will be progressive, and Bank notes may be thrown into circulation, instead of the gold and silver. Besides, there is to be an annual reimbursement of a part of the sum borrowed, which will finally operate as an actual investment of so much specie. In addition to the inducements to this measure, which results from the general interest of the Government, to enlarge the sphere of the utility of the Bank, there is this more particular consideration, to wit, that as far as the dividend on the Stock shall exceed the interest paid on the loan, there is a positive profit.

The Secretary begs leave to conclude, with this general observation, that if the Bank of North America shall come forward with any propositions, which have for object the engrafting upon that institution the characteristics, which shall appear to the Legislature necessary to the due extent and safety of a National Bank, there are, in his judgment, weighty inducements to giving every reasonable facility to the measure. Not only the pretensions of that institution, from its original relation to the Government of the United States, and from the services it has rendered, are such as to claim a disposition favorable to it, if those who are interested in it are willing on their part to place it on a footing satisfactory to the Government, and equal to the purposes of a Bank of the United States; but its cooperation would materially accelerate the accomplishment of the great object, and the collision, which might otherwise arise, might, in a variety of ways, prove equally disagreeable and injurious. The incorporation or union here contemplated, may be effected in different modes, under the auspices of an Act of the United States, if it shall be desired by the Bank of North America, upon terms, which shall appear expedient to the Government.

All which is humbly submitted.

Alexander Hamilton
Secretary of the Treasury

On the Constitutionality of the Bank of the United States

To President George Washington, February 23, 1791

The Secretary of the Treasury having perused with attention the papers containing the opinions of the Secretary of State [Thomas Jefferson] and Attorney General [Edmund Randolph], concerning the constitutionality of the bill for establishing a National Bank, proceeds, according to the order of the President, to submit the reasons which have induced him to entertain a different opinion.

It will naturally have been anticipated, that in performing this task, he would feel uncommon solicitude. Personal considerations alone, arising from the reflection that the measure originated with him, would be sufficient to produce it. The sense which he has manifested of the great importance of such an institution to the successful administration of the department under his particular care, and an expectation of serious ill consequences to result from a failure of the measure, do not permit him to be without anxiety on public accounts. But the chief solicitude arises from a firm persuasion, that principles of construction like those espoused by the Secretary of State and Attorney General, would be fatal to the just and indispensable authority of the United States.

In entering upon the argument, it ought to be premised that the objections of the Secretary of State and Attorney General are founded on a general denial of the authority of the United States to erect corporations. The latter, indeed, expressly admits, that if there be anything in the bill which is not warranted by the Constitution, it is the clause of incorporation.

Now it appears to the Secretary of the Treasury that this *general principle* is *inherent* in the very definition of government, and *essential* to every step of progress to be made by that of the United States, namely: That every power vested in a government is in its nature sovereign, and includes, by *force* of the *term*, a right to employ all the means requisite and fairly applicable to the attainment of the *ends* of such power, and which are not precluded by restrictions and exceptions specified in the Constitution, or not immoral, or not contrary to the essential ends of political society.

This principle, in its application to government in general, would be admitted as an axiom; and it will be incumbent upon those who may incline to deny it, to prove a distinction, and to show that a rule which, in the general system of things, is essential to the preservation of the social order, is inapplicable to the United States.

The circumstance that the powers of sovereignty are in this country divided between the National and State governments, does not afford the distinction required. It does not follow from this, that each of the portion of powers delegated to the one or to the other, is not sovereign with *regard to its proper objects*. It will only follow from it, that each has sovereign power as to *certain things*, and not as to *other things*. To deny that the government of the United States has sovereign power, as to its declared purposes and trusts, because its power does not extend to all cases would be equally to deny that the state governments have sovereign power in any case, because their power does not extend to every case. The tenth section of the first article of the Constitution exhibits a long list of very important things which they may not do. And thus the United States would furnish the singular spectacle of a political society without *sovereignty*, or of a people governed, without government.

If it would be necessary to bring proof to a proposition so clear, as that which affirms that the powers of the federal government, as to its objects, were sovereign, there is a clause of its Constitution which would be decisive. It is that which declares that the Constitution, and the laws of the United States made in pursuance of it, and all treaties made, or which shall be made, under their authority, shall be the *Supreme Law of the land*. The power which can create the supreme law of the land in any case, is doubtless sovereign as to such case.

This general and indisputable principle puts at once an end to the *abstract* question, whether the United States have power to *erect a corporation*; that is to say, to give a *legal* or *artificial capacity* to one or more persons, distinct from the natural. For it is unquestionably incident to sovereign power to erect corporations, and consequently to that of the United States, in *relation* to the *objects* intrusted to the management of the government.

The difference is this: where the authority of the government is general, it can create corporations in *all cases*, where it is confined to certain branches of legislation, it can create corporations only in those cases.

Here then, as far as concerns the reasonings of the Secretary of State and the Attorney General, the affirmative of the constitutionality of the bill might be permitted to rest. It will occur to the President, that the principle here advanced has been untouched by either of them.

For a more complete elucidation of the point, nevertheless, the arguments which they had used against the power of the government to erect corporations, however foreign they are to the great and fundamental rule which has been stated, shall be particularly examined. And after showing that they do not tend to impair its force, it shall also be shown that the power of incorporation, incident to the government in certain cases, does fairly extend to the particular case which is the object of the bill.

The first of these arguments is, that the foundation of the Constitution is laid on this ground: "That all powers not delegated to the United States by the Constitution, nor prohibited to it by the states, are reserved for the states, or to the people." Whence it is meant to be inferred, that Congress can in no case exercise any power not included in those not enumerated in the Constitution. And it is affirmed, that the power of erecting a corporation is not included in any of the enumerated powers.

The main proposition here laid down, in its true signification is not to be questioned. It is nothing more than a consequence of this republican maxim, that all government is a delegation of power. But how much is delegated in each case, is a question of fact, to be made out by fair reasoning and construction, upon the particular provisions of the Constitution, taking as guides the general principles and general ends of governments.

It is not denied that there are implied, as well as *express* powers, and that the former are as effectually delegated as the latter. And for the sake of accuracy it shall be mentioned, that there is another class of powers, which may be properly denominated *resulting* powers. It will not be doubted, that if the United States should make a conquest of any of the territories of its neighbors, they would possess sovereign jurisdiction over the conquered territory. This would be rather a result, from the whole mass of the powers of the government, and from the nature of political society, than a consequence of either of the powers specially enumerated.

But be this as it may, it furnishes a striking illustration of the general doctrine contended for; it shows an extensive case in which a power of erecting corporations is either implied in or would result from, some or all of the powers vested in the national government. The jurisdiction acquired over such conquered country would certainly be competent to any species of legislation.

To return: It is conceded that implied powers are to be considered as delegated equally with express ones.

Then it follows, that as a power of erecting a corporation may as well be *implied* as any other thing, it may as well be employed as an *instrument* or mean of carrying into execution any of the specified powers, as any other instrument or mean whatever. The only question must be in this, as in every other case, whether the mean to be employed or in this instance, the corporation to be erected, has a natural relation to any of the acknowledged objects or lawful ends of the government. Thus a corporation may not be erected by Congress for superintending the police of the city of Philadelphia, because they are not authorized to regulate the police of that city. But one may be erected in relation to the collection of taxes, or to the trade with foreign countries, or to the trade between the states, or with the Indian tribes; because it is the province of the federal government to regulate those objects, and because it is incident to a general *sovereign* or *legislative* power to regulate a thing, to employ all the means which relate to its regulation to the best and greatest advantage.

A strange fallacy seems to have crept into the manner of thinking and reasoning upon the subject. Imagination appears to have been unusually busy concerning it. An incorporation seems to have been regarded as some great independent substantive thing; as a political end of peculiar magnitude and moment; whereas it is truly to be considered as a quality, capacity, or mean to an end. Thus a mercantile company is formed, with a certain capital, for the purpose of carrying on a particular branch of business. Here the business to be prosecuted is the end. The association, in order to form the requisite capital, is the primary mean. Suppose that an incorporation were added to this, it would only be to add a new quality to that association, to give it an artificial capacity, by which it would be enabled to prosecute the business with more safety and convenience.

That the importance of the power of incorporation has been exaggerated, leading to erroneous conclusions, will further appear from tracing it to its origin. The Roman law is the source of it, according to which a voluntary association of individuals, at any time, or for any purpose, was capable of producing it. In England, whence our notions of it are immediately borrowed, it forms part of the executive authority, and the exercise of it has been often delegated by that authority. Whence, therefore, the ground of the supposition that it lies beyond the reach of all those very important portions of sovereign power, legislative as well as executive, which belongs to the government of the United States.

To this mode of reasoning respecting the right of employing all the means requisite to the execution of the specified powers of the government, it is objected, that none but necessary and proper means are to be employed; and the Secretary of State maintains, that no means are to be considered as necessary but those without which the grant of the power would be nugatory. Nay, so far does he go in his restrictive interpretation of the word, as even to make the case of necessity which shall warrant the constitutional exercise of the power to depend on casual and temporary circumstances; an idea which alone refutes the construction. The expediency of exercising a particular power, at a particular time, must, indeed depend on circumstances, but the constitutional right of exercising it must be uniform and invariable, the same to-day as tomorrow.

All the arguments, therefore, against the constitutionality of the bill derived from the accidental existence of certain state banks, institutions which happen to exist to-day, and, for aught that concerns the government of the United States, may disappear tomorrow, must not only be rejected as fallacious, but must be viewed as demonstrative that there is a radical source of error in the reasoning.

It is essential to the being of the national government, that so erroneous a conception of the meaning of the word necessary should be exploded.

It is certain that neither the grammatical nor popular sense of the term requires that construction. According to both, *necessary* often means no more than *needful, requisite, incidental, useful, or conducive to.* It is a common mode of expression to say, that it is necessary for a government or a person to do this or that thing, when nothing more is intended or understood, than that the interests of the government or person require, or will be promoted by, the doing of this or that thing. The imagination can be at no loss for exemplifications of the use of the word in this sense.

And it is the true one in which it is to be understood as used in the Constitution. The whole turn of the clause containing it indicates, that it was the intent of the Convention, by that clause, to give a liberal latitude to the exercise of the specified powers. The expressions have peculiar comprehensiveness. They are—To make all laws necessary and proper for *carrying into execution the foregoing powers, and all other powers* vested by the Constitution in the government of the United States, or in any *department* or officer thereof. To understand the word as the Secretary of State does, would be to depart from its obvious and popular sense, and to give it a *restrictive* operation, an idea never before entertained. It would be to give it the same force as if the word *absolutely* or *indispensably* had been prefixed to it.

Such a construction would beget endless uncertainty and embarrassment. The cases must be palpable and extreme, in which it could be pronounced, with certainty, that a measure was absolutely necessary, or one, without which, the exercise of a given power would be nugatory. There are few measures of any government which would stand so severe a test. To insist upon it, would be to make the criterion of the exercise of any implied power, a *case of extreme necessity*; which is rather a rule to justify the overleaping of the bounds of constitutional authority, than to govern the ordinary exercise of it.

It may be truly said of every government, as well as of that of the United States, that it has only a right to pass such laws as are necessary and proper to accomplish the objects entrusted to it. For no government has a right to do *merely what it pleases*. Hence, by a process of reasoning similar to that of the Secretary of State, it might be proved that neither of the state governments has a right to incorporate a bank. It might be shown that all the public business of the state could be performed without a bank, and inferring thence that it was unnecessary, it might be argued that it could not be done, because it is against the rule which has been just mentioned.

A like mode of reasoning would prove that there was no power to incorporate the inhabitants of a town, with a view to a more perfect police. For it is certain that an incorporation may be dispensed with, though it is better to have one. It is to be remembered that there is no express power in any state constitution to erect corporations.

The degree in which a measure is necessary, can never be a test of the *legal right* to adopt it; that must be a matter of opinion, and can only be a test of expediency. The relation between the *measure* and the *end*; between the *nature* of the *mean* employed toward the execution of a power, and the *object* of that power must be the criterion of constitutionality, not the more or less of necessity or utility.

The practice of the government is against the rule of construction advocated by the Secretary of State. Of this, the Act concerning lighthouses, beacons, buoys, and public piers, is a decisive example. This, doubtless, must be referred to the powers of regulating trade, and is fairly relative to it. But it cannot be affirmed that the exercise of that power in this instance was strictly necessity or that the power itself would be *nugatory*, without that of regulating establishments of this nature.

This restrictive interpretation of the word *necessary* is also contrary to this sound maxim of construction, namely, that the powers contained in a constitution of government, especially those which concern the general administration of the affairs of a country, its finances, trade, defense, etc., ought to be construed liberally in advancement of the public good. This rule does not depend on the particular form of a government, or on the particular demarcation of the boundaries of its powers, but on the nature and object of government itself. The means by which national exigencies are to be provided for, national inconveniences obviated, national prosperity promoted, are of such infinite variety, extent, and complexity, that there must of necessity be great latitude of discretion in the selection and application of those means. Hence, consequently, the necessity and propriety of exercising the authorities entrusted to a government on principles of liberal construction.

The Attorney General admits the *rule*, but takes a distinction between a state and the Federal Constitution. The latter, he thinks, ought to be construed with greater strictness, because there is more danger of error in defining partial than general powers.

But the reason of the *rule* forbids such a distinction. This reason is—The variety and extent of public exigencies, a far greater proportion of which, and of a far more critical kind, are objects of National than of State administration. The greater danger of error, as far as it is supposable, may be a prudential reason for caution in practice, but it cannot be a rule of restrictive interpretation.

In regard to the clause of the Constitution immediately under consideration, it is admitted by the Attorney General, that no restrictive effect can be ascribed to it. He defines the word necessary thus: "To be necessary is to be *incidental*, and may be denominated the natural means of executing a power."

But while on the one hand the construction of the Secretary of State is deemed inadmissible, it will not be contended, on the other, that the clause in question gives any new or independent power. But it gives an explicit sanction to the doctrine of implied powers, and is equivalent to an admission of the proposition that the government, *as to its specified powers* and *objects*, has plenary and sovereign authority, in some cases paramount to the states; in others, co-ordinate with it. For such is the plain import of the declaration, that it may pass all LAWS necessary and proper to carry into execution those powers.

It is no valid objection to the doctrine to say, that it is calculated to extend the power of the government throughout the entire sphere of state legislation. The same thing has been said, and may be said, with regard to every exercise of power by *implication* or *construction*. The moment the literal meaning is departed from, there is a chance of error and abuse. And yet an adherence to the letter of its powers would at once arrest the motions of government. It is not only agreed, on all hands, that the exercise of constructive powers is indispensable, but every act which has been passed, is more or less an exemplification of it. One has been already mentioned that relating to lighthouses, etc. That which declares the power of the President to remove officers at pleasure, acknowledges the same truth in another and a signal instance.

The truth is, that difficulties on this point are inherent in the nature of the Federal Constitution; they result inevitably from a division of the legislative power. The consequence of this division is, that there will be cases clearly within the power of the national government; others, clearly without its powers; and a third class, which will leave room for controversy and difference of opinion, and concerning which a reasonable latitude of judgment must be allowed.

But the doctrine which is contended for is not chargeable with the consequences imputed to it. It does not affirm that the national government is sovereign in all respects, but that it is sovereign to a certain extent; that is, to the extent of the objects of its specified powers.

It leaves, therefore, a criterion of what is constitutional, and of what is not so. This criterion is the end, to which the measure relates as a mean. If the end be clearly comprehended within any of the specified powers, and if the measure have an obvious relation to that end, and is not forbidden by any particular provision of the Constitution, it may safely be deemed to come within the compass of the national authority. There is also this further criterion, which may materially assist the decision: Does the proposed measure abridge a pre-existing right of any state or of any individual? If it does not, there is a strong presumption in favor of its constitutionality, and slighter relations to any declared object of the Constitution may be permitted to turn the scale.

The general objections, which are to be inferred from the reasonings of the Secretary of State and Attorney General, to the doctrine which has been advanced, have been stated, and it is hoped satisfactorily answered. Those of a more particular nature shall now be examined.

The Secretary of State introduces his opinion with an observation, that the proposed incorporation undertakes to create certain capacities, properties, or attributes, which are against the laws of alienage, descents, *escheat* and *forfeiture*, distribution and monopoly, and to confer a power to make laws paramount to those of the states. And nothing, says he, in another place, but *necessity*, invincible by other means, can justify such a prostration of laws, which constitute the pillars of our whole system of jurisprudence, and are the foundation laws of the state governments.

If these are truly the foundation laws of the several states, then have most of them subverted their own foundations. For there is scarcely one of them which has not, since the establishment of its particular constitution, made material alterations in some of those branches of its jurisprudence, especially the law of descents. But it is not conceived how anything can be called the fundamental law of a state government which is not established in its constitution unalterable by the ordinary legislature. And, with regard to the question of necessity, it has been shown that this can only constitute a question of expediency, not of right.

To erect a corporation, is to substitute a legal or *artificial* for a *natural* person, and where a *number* are concerned, to give them *individuality*. To that legal or artificial person, once created, the common law of every state, of itself, annexes all those incidents and attributes which are represented as a prostration of the main pillars of their jurisprudence.—It is certainly not accurate to say, that the erection of a corporation is *against* those different *heads* of the state laws; because it is rather to create a kind of person or entity, to which they are inapplicable, and to which the general rule of those laws assign a different regimen. The laws of alienage cannot apply to an artificial person, because it can have no country; those of descent cannot apply to it, because it can have no heirs; those of escheat are foreign from it, for the same reason; those of forfeiture, because it cannot commit a crime; those of distribution, because, though it may be dissolved, it cannot die. As truly might it be said, that the exercise of the power of prescribing the rule by which foreigners shall be naturalized, is against the law of alienage, while it is, in fact, only to put them in a situation to cease to be the subject of that law. To do a thing which is against a law, is to do something which it forbids, or which is a violation of it.

But if it were even to be admitted that the erection of a corporation is a direct alteration of the state laws, in the enumerated particulars, it would do nothing toward proving that the measure was unconstitutional. If the government of the United States can do no act which amounts to an alteration of a state law, all its powers are nugatory; for almost every new law is an alteration, in same way or other, of an *old law*, either common or statute.

There are laws concerning bankruptcy in some states. Some states have laws regulating the values of foreign coins. Congress are empowered to establish uniform laws concerning bankruptcy throughout the United States, and to regulate the values of foreign coins. The exercise of either of these powers by Congress, necessarily involves an alteration of the laws of those states.

Again—Every person, by the common law of each state, may export his property to foreign countries, at pleasure; but Congress, in pursuance of the power of regulating trade, may prohibit the exportation of commodities; in doing which, they would alter the common law of each state, in abridgment of individual right.

It can therefore never be good reasoning to say this or that act is unconstitutional, because it alters this or that law of a state. It must be shown that the act which makes the alteration is unconstitutional on other accounts, not *because* it makes the alteration.

There are two points in the suggestions of the Secretary of State, which have been noted, that are peculiarly incorrect. One is, that the proposed incorporation is against the laws of monopoly, because it stipulates an exclusive right of banking under the national authority; the other, that it gives power to the institution to make laws paramount to those of the states.

But, with regard to the first: The bill neither prohibits any state from erecting as many banks as they please, nor any number of individuals from associating to carry on the business, and consequently, is free from the charge of establishing a monopoly; for monopoly implies a *legal impediment* to the carrying on of the trade by others than those to whom it is granted.

And with regard to the second point, there is still less foundation. The by-laws of such an institution as a bank can operate only on its own members, can only concern the disposition of its own property, and must essentially resemble the rules of a private mercantile partnership. They are expressly not to be contrary to law; and law must here mean the law of a state, as well as of the United States. There never can be a doubt, that a law of a corporation, if contrary to a law of a state, must be overruled as void unless the law of the state is contrary to that of the United States and then the question will not be between the law of the state and that of the corporation, but between the law of the state and that of the United States.

Another argument made use of by the Secretary of State is, the rejection of a proposition by the Convention to empower Congress to make corporations, either generally, or for some special purpose. What was the precise nature or extent of this proposition, or what the reasons for refusing it, is not ascertained by any authentic document, or even by accurate recollection. As far as any such document exists, it specifies only canals. If this was the amount of it, it would, at most, only prove that it was thought inexpedient to give a power to incorporate for the purpose of opening canals, for which purpose a special power would have been necessary, except with regard to the western territory, there being nothing in any part of the Constitution respecting the regulation of canals. It must be confessed, however, that very different accounts are given of the import of the proposition, and of the motives for rejecting it. Some affirm, that it was confined to the opening of canals and obstructions in rivers, others, that it embraced banks; and others, that it extended to the power of incorporating generally. Some, again, allege, that it was disagreed to because it was thought improper to vest in Congress a power of erecting corporations. Others, because it was thought unnecessary to specify the power, and inexpedient to furnish an additional topic of objection to the Constitution. In this state of the matter, no inference whatever can be drawn from it.

But whatever may have been the nature of the proposition, or the reasons for rejecting it, nothing is included by it, that is the proposition, in respect to the real merits of the question. The Secretary of State will not deny, that, whatever may have been the intention of the framers of a constitution, or of a law, that intention is to be sought for in the instrument itself, according to the usual and established rules of construction. Nothing is more common than for laws to *express* and *effect* more or less than was intended. If, then, a power to erect a corporation in any case be deducible, by fair inference, from the whole or any part of the numerous provisions of the Constitution of the United States, arguments drawn from extrinsic circumstances regarding the intention of the Convention must be rejected.

Most of the arguments of the Secretary of State, which have not been considered in the foregoing remarks, are of a nature rather to apply to the expediency than to the constitutionality of the bill. They will, however, be noticed in the discussions which will be necessary in reference to the particular heads of the powers of the government which are involved in the question.

Those of the Attorney General will now properly come under view.

His first objection is, that the power of incorporation is not *expressly* given to Congress. This shall be conceded, but in this sense only, that it is not declared in *express terms* that Congress may erect a corporation. But this cannot mean, that there are not certain express powers which necessarily include it.

For instance Congress have express power to exercise exclusive legislation in all cases whatsoever, over such district (not exceeding ten miles square) as may, by cession of particular states and the acceptance of Congress, become the seat of the government of the United States; and to exercise like authority over all places purchased, by consent of the legislature of the state in which the same shall be for the erection of forts, arsenals, dockyards, and other needful buildings.

Here, then, is express power to exercise exclusive *legislation, in all cases whatsoever, over certain places*; that is to do, in respect to those places, all that any government whatsoever may do. For language does not afford a more complete designation of sovereign power than in those comprehensive terms. It is, in other words, a power to pass all laws whatsoever, and consequently, to pass laws for erecting corporations, as well as for any other purpose which is the proper object of law in a free government. Surely it can never be believed that Congress, with *exclusive powers of legislation in all cases whatsoever*, cannot erect a corporation within the district which shall become the seat of government, for the better regulation of its police. And yet there is an unqualified denial of the power to erect corporations in every case on the part both of the Secretary of State and of the Attorney General; the former, indeed, speaks of that power in these emphatical terms: That it is a *right remaining exclusively with the states.*

As far, then, as there is an express power to do any *particular* act of *legislation*, there is an express one to erect a corporation in the case above described. But, accurately speaking, *no particular power* is more than that *implied* in a general one. Thus the power to lay a duty on a *gallon of rum* is only a particular *implied* in the general power to collect taxes, duties, imposts, and excises. This serves to explain in what sense it may be said that Congress have not an express power to make corporations.

This may not be an improper place to take notice of an argument which was used in debate in the House of Representatives. It was there argued, that if the Constitution intended to confer so important a power as that of erecting corporations, it would have been expressly mentioned. But the case which has been noticed is clearly one in which such a power exists, and yet without any specification of express grant of it, further than as every *particular implied* in a general power can be said to be so granted.

But the argument itself is founded upon an exaggerated and erroneous conception of the nature of the power. It has been shown that it is not of so transcendent a kind as the reasoning supposes, and that, viewed in a just light, it is a mean which ought to have been left to *implication*, rather than an end which ought to have been *expressly* granted.

Having observed that the power of erecting corporations is not expressly granted to Congress, the Attorney General proceeds thus:

If it can be exercised by them, it must be

1. Because the nature of the federal government implies it.

2. Because it is involved in some of the specified powers of legislation.

3. Because it is necessary and proper to carry into execution some of the specified powers.

To be implied in the nature of the federal government, says he, would beget a doctrine so indefinite as to grasp every power.

This proposition, it ought to be remarked, is not precisely, or even substantially, that which has been relied upon. The proposition relied upon is, that the *specified powers of Congress* are in their nature sovereign. That it is incident to sovereign power to erect corporations, and that therefore Congress have a right, within the *sphere and in relation to the objects of their power, to erect corporations.*

It shall, however, be supposed that the Attorney General would consider the two propositions in the same light, and that the objection made to the one would be made to the other.

To this objection an answer has been already given. It is this, that the doctrine is stated with this express *qualification*, that the right to erect corporations does only extend to *cases* and *objects* within the *sphere* of the *specified* powers of the government. A general legislative authority implies a power to erect corporations in all cases. A particular legislative power implies authority to erect corporations in relation to cases arising under that power only. Hence the affirming that, as incident to sovereign power, Congress may erect a corporation in relation to the collection of their taxes, is no more to affirm that they may do whatever else they please, than the saying that they have a power to regulate trade, would be to affirm that they have a power to regulate religion; or than the maintaining that they have sovereign *power* as to taxation, would be to maintain that they have sovereign power as to everything else.

The Attorney General undertakes in the next place to show, that the power of erecting corporations is not involved in any of the specified powers of legislation confided to the national government.

In order to [do] this, he has attempted an enumeration of the particulars which he supposes to be comprehended under the several heads of the POWERS to lay and collect taxes, etc.; to borrow money on the credit of the United States, to regulate commerce with sovereign nations, between the states, and with the Indian tribes, to dispose of and make all needful rules and regulations respecting the territory or other property belonging to the United States. The design of which enumeration is to show, *what is* included under those different heads of power, and negatively, that the power of erecting corporations is not included.

The truth of this inference or conclusion must depend on the accuracy of the enumeration. If it can be shown that the enumeration is defective, the inference is destroyed. To do this will be attended with no difficulty.

The heads of the power to lay and collect taxes are stated to be:

1. To ascertain the subjects of taxation, etc.
2. To declare the quantum of taxation, etc.
3. To prescribe the mode of collection.
4. To ordain the manner of accounting for the taxes, etc.

The defectiveness of this enumeration consists in the generality of the third division, "to *prescribe the mode of collection*," which is in itself an immense chapter. It will be shown hereafter, that among a vast variety of particulars, it comprises the very power in question, namely, to *erect corporations*.

The heads of the power to borrow money, are stated to be:

1. To stipulate the sum to be lent.
2. An interest or no interest to be paid.
3. The time and manner of repaying, unless the loan be placed on an irredeemable fund.

This enumeration is liable to a variety of objections. It omits in the first place, the *pledging* or *mortgaging* of a fund for the security of the money lent, an usual, and in most cases an essential ingredient.

The idea of a stipulation of an *interest* or *no interest* is too confined. It should rather have been said, to stipulate the consideration of the loan. Individuals often borrow on considerations other than the payment of interest, so may governments, and so they often find it necessary to do. Everyone recollects the lottery tickets and other douceurs often given in Great Britain as collateral inducements to the lending of money to the government.

There are also frequently collateral conditions, which the enumeration does not contemplate. Every contract which has been made for moneys borrowed in Holland, includes stipulations that the sum due shall be *free from taxes*, and from sequestration in time of war, and mortgages all the land and property of the United States for the reimbursement.

It is also known that a lottery is a common expedient for borrowing money, which certainly does not fall under either of the enumerated heads.

The heads of the power to regulate commerce with foreign

nations, are stated to be:

1. To prohibit them or their commodities from our ports.

2. To impose duties on them, where none existed before, or to increase existing duties on them.

3. To subject them to any species of customhouse regulation.

4. To grant them any exemptions or privileges which policy may suggest.

This enumeration is far more exceptionable than either of the former. It omits *every thing* that relates to the *citizens*, vessels, or commodities of the United States.

The following palpable omissions occur at once:

1. Of the power to prohibit the exportation of commodities, which not only exists at all times, but which in time of war it would be necessary to exercise, particularly with relation to naval and warlike stores.

2. Of the power to prescribe rules concerning the characteristics and privileges of an American bottom, how she shall be navigated, or whether by citizens or foreigners, or by a proportion of each.

3. Of the power of regulating the manner of contracting with seamen; the police of ships on their voyages, etc., of which the act for the government and regulation of seamen, in the merchants' service, is a specimen.

That the three preceding articles are omissions, will not be doubted there is a long list of items in addition, which admit of little, if any question, of which a few samples shall be given.

1. The granting of bounties to certain kinds of vessels, and certain species of merchandise; of this nature, is the allowance on dried and pickled fish and salted provisions

2. The prescribing of rules concerning the inspection of commodities to be exported. Though the states individually are competent to this regulation, yet there is no reason, in point of authority at least, why a general system might not be adopted by the United States.

3. The regulation of policies of insurance; of salvage upon

goods found at sea, and the disposition of such goods.

4. The regulation of pilots.

5. The regulation of bills of exchange drawn by a merchant of *one state* upon a merchant of *another* state. This last rather belongs to the regulation of trade between the states, but is equally omitted in the specifications under that head.

The last enumeration relates to the power to dispose of, and make *all needful* rules and regulations respecting the territory or *other property* belonging to the United States.

The heads of this power are said to be:

1. To exert an ownership over the territory of the United States which may be properly called the property of the United States, as in the western territory, and to *institute a government* therein; or,

2. To exert an ownership over the other property of the United States.

The idea of exerting an ownership over the territory or other property of the United States, is particularly indefinite and vague. It does not at all satisfy the conception of what must have been intended by a power to make all needful *rules* and *regulations*, nor would there have been any use for a special clause, which authorized nothing more. For the right of exerting an ownership is implied in the very definition of property.

It is admitted, that in regard to the western territory, something more is intended; even the institution of a government, that is, the creation of a body politic, or corporation of the highest nature; one which, in its maturity, will be able itself to create other corporations. Why, then, does not the same clause authorize the erection of a corporation, in respect to the regulation or disposal of any other of the property of the United States.

This idea will be enlarged upon in another place.

Hence it appears, that the enumerations which have been attempted by the Attorney General, are so imperfect, as to authorize no conclusion whatever; they, therefore, have no tendency to disprove that each and every of the powers, to which they relate, includes that of erecting corporations, which they certainly do, as the subsequent illustrations will more and more evince.

It is presumed to have been satisfactorily shown in the course of the preceding observations:

1. That the power of the government, as to the objects intrusted to its management, is, in its nature, sovereign.

2. That the right of erecting corporations is one inherent in, and inseparable from, the idea of sovereign power.

3. That the position, that the government of the United States can exercise no power, but such as is delegated to it by its Constitution, does not militate against this principle.

4. That the word *necessary*, in the general clause, can have no *restrictive* operation derogating from the force of this principle; indeed, that the degree in which a measure is or is not necessary cannot be a *test* of *constitutional* right, but of expediency only.

5. That the power to erect corporations is not to be considered as an independent or substantive power, but as an incidental and auxiliary one, and was therefore more properly left to implication, than expressly granted.

6. That the principle in question does not extend the power of the government beyond the prescribed limits, because it only affirms a power to incorporate for purposes *within the sphere of the specified powers.*

And lastly, that the right to exercise such a power in certain cases is unequivocally granted in the most positive and comprehensive terms.

To all which it only remains to be added, that such a power has actually been exercised in two very eminent instances, namely, in the erection of two governments, one north-west of the River Ohio, and the other south-west, the last independent of any antecedent compact.

And there results a full and complete demonstration that the Secretary of State and the Attorney General are mistaken when they deny generally the power of the national government to erect corporations.

It shall now be endeavored to be shown that there is a power to erect one of the kind proposed by the bill. This will be done by tracing a natural and obvious relation between the institution of a bank and the objects of several of the enumerated powers of the government; and by showing that, *politically* speaking, it is necessary to the effectual execution of one or more of those powers. In the course of this investigation, various instances will be stated, by way of illustration of a right to erect corporations under those powers.

Some preliminary observations may be proper.

The proposed bank is to consist of an association of persons, for the purpose of creating a joint capital, to be employed chiefly and essentially in loans. So far the object is not only lawful, but it is the mere exercise of a right which the law allows to every individual. The Bank of New York, which is not incorporated, is an example of such an association. The bill proposes, in addition, that the government shall become a joint proprietor in this undertaking, and that it shall permit the bills of the company, payable on demand, to be receivable in its revenues; and stipulates that it shall not grant privileges, similar to those which are to be allowed to this company, to any others. All this is incontrovertibly within the compass of the discretion of the government. The only question is, whether it has a right to incorporate this company, in order to enable it the more effectually to accomplish ends which are in themselves lawful.

To establish such a right, it remains to show the relation of such an institution to one or more of the specified powers of the government.

Accordingly, it is affirmed that it has a relation, more or less direct, to the power of collecting taxes, to that of borrowing money, to that of regulating trade between the states, and to those of raising and maintaining fleets and armies. To the two former, the relation may be said to be immediate.

And in the last place it will be argued, that it is clearly within the provision which authorizes the making of all *needful rules* and *regulations* concerning the property of the United States, as the same has been practiced upon by the government.

A bank relates to the collection of taxes in two ways. *Indirectly*, by increasing the quantity of circulating medium and quickening circulation, which facilitates the means of paying; *directly*, by creating a *convenient species* of medium in which they are to be paid.

To designate or appoint the money or thing in which taxes are to be paid, is not only a proper, but a necessary exercise of the power of collecting them. Accordingly, Congress, in the law concerning the collection of the duties on imposts and tonnage, have provided that they shall be paid in gold and silver. But while it was an indispensable part of the work to say in what they should be paid, the choice of the specific thing was mere matter of discretion. The payment might have been required in the commodities themselves. Taxes in kind, however ill-judged, are not without precedents, even in the United States; or it might have been in the paper money of the several states, or in the bills of the Bank of North America, New York and Massachusetts, all or either of them; or it might have been in bills issued under the authority of the United States.

No part of this can, it is presumed, be disputed. The appointment, then, of the money or thing in which the taxes are to be paid, is an incident to the power of collection. And among the expedients which may be adopted, is that of bills issued under the authority of the United States.

Now, the manner of issuing these bills is again matter of discretion. The government might doubtless proceed in the following manner: It might provide that they should be issued under the direction of certain officers, payable on demand, and, in order to support their credit, and give them a ready circulation, it might, besides giving them a currency in its taxes, set apart, out of any moneys in its treasury, a given sum, and appropriate it, under the direction of those officers, as a fund for answering the bills, as presented for payment.

The constitutionality of all this would not admit of a question, and yet it would amount to the institution of a bank, with a view to the more convenient collection of taxes. For the simplest and most precise idea of a bank is, a deposit of coin, or other property, as a fund for circulating credit upon it, which is to answer the purpose of money. That such an arrangement would be equivalent to the establishment of a bank, would become obvious if the place where the fund to be set apart was kept should be made a receptacle of the moneys of all other persons who should incline to deposit them there for safe-keeping; and would become still more so, if the officers charged with the direction of the fund were authorized to make discounts at the usual rate of interest, upon good security. To deny the power of the government to add these ingredients to the plan, would be to refine away all government.

A further process will still more clearly illustrate the point. Suppose, when the species of bank which has been described was about to be instituted, it was to be urged that, in order to secure to it a due degree of confidence, the fund ought not only to be set apart and appropriated generally, but ought to be specifically vested in the officers who were to have the direction of it, and in their successors in office, to the end that it might acquire the character of *private property*, incapable of being resumed without a violation of the sanctions by which the rights of property are protected, and occasioning more serious and general alarm: the apprehension of which might operate as a check upon the government. Such a proposition might be opposed by arguments against the expedience of it, or the solidity of the reason assigned for it, but it is not conceivable what could be urged against its constitutionality.

And yet such a disposition of the thing would amount to the erection of a corporation; for the true definition of a corporation seems to be this: It is a *legal* person, or a person created by act of law, consisting of one or more natural persons authorized to hold property, or a franchise in succession, in a legal, as contradistinguished from natural, capacity.

Let the illustration proceed a step further. Suppose a bank of the nature which has been described, with or without incorporation, had been instituted, and that experience had evinced as it probably would, that, being wholly under a public direction, it possessed not the confidence requisite to the credit of the bills. Suppose, also, that, by some of those adverse conjunctures which occasionally attend nations, there had been a very great drain of the specie of the country, so as not only to cause general distress for want of an adequate medium of circulation, but to produce, in consequence of that circumstance, considerable defalcations in the public revenues. Suppose, also, that there was no bank instituted in any state; in such a posture of things, would it not be most manifest, that the incorporation of a bank like that proposed by the bill would be a measure immediately relative to the effectual collection of the taxes, and completely within the province of the sovereign power of providing, by all laws necessary and proper, for that collection?

If it be said, that such a state of things would render that necessary, and therefore constitutional, which is not so now, the answer to this, (and a solid one it doubtless is,) must still be, that which has been already stated; circumstances may affect the expediency of the measure, but they can neither add to nor diminish its *constitutionality*.

A bank has a direct relation to the power of borrowing money, because it is an usual, and in sudden emergencies, an essential, instrument in the obtaining of loans to government.

A nation is threatened with a war, large sums are wanted on a sudden to make the requisite preparations. Taxes are laid for the purpose, but it requires tine to obtain the benefit of them. Anticipation is indispensable. If there be a bank, the supply can at once be had. If there be none, loans from individuals must be sought. The progress of these is often too slow for the exigency; in some situations they are not practicable at all. Frequently when they are, it is of great consequence to be able to anticipate the product of them by advance from a bank.

The essentiality of such an institution as an instrument of loans is exemplified at this very moment. An Indian expedition is to be prosecuted. The only fund, out of which the money can arise, consistently with the public engagements, is a tax, which only begins to be collected in July next. The preparations, however, are instantly to be made. The money must, therefore, be borrowed; and of whom could it be borrowed, if there were no public banks ?

It happens that there are institutions of this kind, but if there were none, it would be indispensable to create one.

Let it then be supposed that the necessity existed, (as but for a casualty would be the case,) that proposals were made for obtaining a loan; that a number of individuals came forward and said, we are willing to accommodate the government with the money; with what we have in hand, and the credit we can raise upon it, we doubt not of being able to furnish the sum required; but in order to this, it is indispensable that we should be incorporated as a bank. This is essential toward putting it in our power to do what is desired, and we are obliged on that account to make it the *consideration* or *condition* of the loan.

Can it be believed that a compliance with this proposition would be unconstitutional? Does not this alone evince the contrary? It is a necessary part of a power to borrow, to be able to stipulate the consideration or conditions of a loan. It is evident, as has been remarked elsewhere, that this is not confined to the mere stipulation of a franchise. If it may, and it is not perceived why it may not, then the grant of a corporate capacity may be stipulated as a consideration of the loan. There seems to be nothing unfit or foreign from the nature of the thing in giving individuality, or a corporate capacity to a number of persons, who are willing to lend a sum of money to the government, the better to enable them to do it, and make them an ordinary instrument of loans in future emergencies of the state.

But the more general view of the subject is still more satisfactory. The legislative power of borrowing money, and of making all laws necessary and proper for carrying into execution that power, seems obviously competent to the appointment of the organ, through which the abilities and wills of individuals may be most efficaciously exerted for the accommodation of the government by loans.

The Attorney General opposes to this reasoning the following observation: "Borrowing money presupposes the accumulation of a fund to be lent, and is secondary to the creation of an ability to lend." This is plausible in theory, but is not true in fact. In a great number of cases, a previous accumulation of a fund equal to the whole sum required does not exist. And nothing more can be actually presupposed, than that there exist resources, which, put into activity to the greatest advantage by the nature of the operation with the government, will be equal to the effect desired to be produced. All the provisions and operations of government must be presumed to contemplate things as they *really* are.

The institution of a bank has also a natural relation to the regulation of trade between the states, in so far as it is conducive to the creation of a convenient medium of exchange between them, and to the keeping up a full circulation, by preventing the frequent displacement of the metals in reciprocal remittances. Money is the very hinge on which commerce turns. And this does not merely mean gold and silver; many other things have served the purpose, with different degrees of utility. Paper has been extensively employed.

It cannot, therefore, be admitted, with the Attorney General, that the regulation of trade between the states, as it concerns the medium of circulation and exchange, ought to be considered as confined to coin. It is even supposable that the whole or the greatest part, of the coin of the country might be carried out of it.

The Secretary of State objects to the relation here insisted upon by the following mode of reasoning: To erect a bank, says he, and to regulate commerce, are very different acts. He who creates a bank, creates a subject of commerce, so does he who raises a bushel of wheat, or digs a dollar out of the mines, yet neither of these persons regulates commerce thereby. To make a thing which may be bought and sold, is not to prescribe regulations for *buying* and *selling*. This is making the regulation of commerce to consist in prescribing rules for buying and selling.

This, indeed, is a species of regulation of trade, but is one which falls more aptly within the province of the local jurisdictions, than within that of the general government, whose care they must be presumed to have been intended to be directed to those general political arrangements concerning trade, on which its aggregated interests depend, rather than to the details of buying and selling.

Accordingly, such only are the regulations to be found in the laws of the United States; whose objects are to give encouragement to the enterprise of our own merchants, and to advance our navigation and manufactures.

And it is in reference to these general relations of commerce, that an establishment which furnishes facilities to circulation, and a convenient medium of exchange and alienation, is to be regarded as a regulation of trade.

The Secretary of State further argues, that if this was a regulation of commerce, it would be void, as extending as much to the internal commerce of every state as to its external. But what regulation of commerce does not extend to the internal commerce of every state? What are all the duties upon imported articles amounting to prohibitions, but so many bounties upon domestic manufactures, affecting the interests of different classes of citizens, in different ways? What are all the provisions in the coasting act which relate to the trade between district and district of the same state? In short, what regulation of trade between the states, but must affect the internal trade of each state? What can operate upon the whole, but must extend to every part ?

The relation of a bank to the execution of the powers that concern the common defense has been anticipated. It has been noted, that, at this very moment, the aid of such an institution is essential to the measures to be pursued for the protection of our frontiers.

It now remains to show, that the incorporation of a bank is within the operation of the provision which authorizes Congress to make all needful rules and regulations concerning the property of the United States. But it is previously necessary to advert to a distinction which has been taken by the Attorney General.

He admits that the word property may signify personal property, however acquired, and yet asserts that it cannot signify money arising from the sources of revenue pointed out in the Constitution, "because," says he, "the disposal and regulation of money is the final cause for raising it by taxes."

But it would be more accurate to say that the *object* to which money is intended to be applied is the *final cause* for raising it, than that the disposal and regulation of it is such. The support of government—the support of troops for the common defense— the payment of the public debt, are the true final causes for raising money. The disposition and regulation of it, when raised, are the steps by which it is applied to the *ends* for which it was raised, not the ends themselves. Hence, therefore, the money to be raised by taxes, as well as any other personal property, must be supposed to come within the meaning, as they certainly do within the letter, of authority to make all needful rules and regulations concerning the property of the United States.

A case will make this plainer. Suppose the public debt discharged, and the funds now pledged for it liberated. In some instances it would be found expedient to repeal the taxes; in others, the repeal might injure our own industry, our agriculture and manufactures. In these cases they would, of course, be retained. Here, then, would be moneys arising from the authorized sources of revenue, which would not fall within the rule by which the Attorney General endeavors to except them from other personal property, and from the operation of the clause in question.

The moneys being in the coffers of government, what is to hinder such a disposition to be made of them as is contemplated in the bill, or what an incorporation of the parties concerned, under the clause which has been cited?

It is admitted that with regard to the western territory they give a power to erect a corporation that is, to institute a government; and by what rule of construction can it be maintained, that the same words in a constitution of government will not have the same effect when applied to one species of property as to another as far as the subject is capable of it? Or that a legislative power to make all needful rules and regulations, or to pass all laws necessary and proper, concerning the public property, which is admitted to authorize an incorporation in one case, will not authorize it in another? will justify the institution of a government over the western territory, and will not justify the incorporation of a bank for the more useful management of the moneys of the United States? If it will do the last, as well as the first, then under this provision alone, the bill is constitutional, because it contemplates that the United States shall be joint proprietors of the stock of the bank.

There is an observation of the Secretary of State to this effect which may require notice in this place: Congress, says he, are not to lay taxes ad libitum, *for any purpose they please*, but only to pay the debts or provide for the welfare of the Union. Certainly no inference can be drawn from this against the power of applying their money for the institution of a bank. It is true that they cannot without breach of trust lay taxes for any other purpose than the general welfare; but so neither can any other government. The welfare of the community is the only legitimate end for which money can be raised on the community. Congress can be considered as under only one restriction which does not apply to other governments—they cannot rightfully apply the money they raise to any purpose merely or purely local. But, with this exception, they have as large a discretion in relation to the application of money as any legislature whatever.

The constitutional *test* of a right application must always be, whether it be for a purpose of general or local nature. If the former, there can be no want of constitutional power. The quality of the object, as how far it will really promote, or not, the welfare of the Union must be matter of conscientious discretion; and the arguments for or against a measure, in this light, must be arguments concerning expediency; or inexpediency, not constitutional right; whatever relates to the general order of the finances, to the general interests of trade, etc., being general objects, are constitutional ones for the *application of money.*

A bank, then, whose bills are to circulate in all the revenues of the country, is evidently a general object, and, for that very reason, a constitutional one, as far as regards the appropriation of money to it. Whether it will really be a beneficial one or not, is worthy of careful examination, but is no more a constitutional point, in the particular referred to, than the question, whether the western lands shall be sold for twenty or thirty cents per acre.

A hope is entertained that it has, by this time, been made to appear, to the satisfaction of the President, that a bank has a natural relation to the power of collecting taxes—to that of regulating trade—to that of providing for the common defense and that, as the bill under consideration contemplates the government in the light of a joint proprietor of the stock of the bank, it brings the case within the provision of the clause of the Constitution which immediately respects the property of the United States.

Under a conviction that such a relation subsists, the Secretary of the Treasury, with all deference, conceives, that it will result as a necessary consequence, from the position that all the special powers of government are sovereign, as to the proper objects, that the incorporation of a bank is a constitutional measure: and that the objections taken to the bill, in this respect, are ill-founded.

But, from an earnest desire to give the utmost possible satisfaction to the mind of the President, on so delicate and important a subject, the Secretary of the Treasury will ask his indulgence, while he gives some additional illustrations of cases in which a power of erecting corporations may be exercised, under some of those heads of the specified powers of the government, which are alleged to include the right of incorporating a bank.

I.   It does not appear susceptible of a doubt, that if Congress had thought proper to provide, in the collection laws, that the bonds to be given for the duties, should be given to the collector of the district of A. or B. as the case might require, to enure to him and his successors in office, in trust for the United States, that it would have been consistent with the Constitution to make such an arrangement; and yet this, it is conceived, would amount to an incorporation.

II.   It is not an unusual expedient of taxation to farm particular branches of revenue—that is, to mortgage or sell the product of them for certain definite sums, leaving the collection to the parties to whom they are mortgaged or sold. There are even examples of this in the United States. Suppose that there was any particular branch of revenue which it was manifestly expedient to place on this footing, and there were a number of persons willing to engage with the government, upon condition that they should be incorporated, and the sums invested in them, as well for their greater safety, as for the more convenient recovery and management of the taxes. Is it supposable that there could be any constitutional obstacle to the measure? It is presumed that there could be none. It is certainly a mode of collection which it would be in the discretion of the government to adopt, though the circumstances must be very extraordinary, that would induce the Secretary to think it expedient.

III. Suppose a new and unexplored branch of trade should present itself, with some foreign country. Suppose it was manifest that to undertake it with advantage required an union of the capitals of a number of individuals, and that those individuals would not be disposed to embark without an incorporation, as well to obviate that consequence of a private partnership which makes every individual liable in his whole estate for the debts of the company, to their utmost extent, as for the more convenient management of the business—what reason can there be to doubt that the national government would have a constitutional right to institute and incorporate such a company? None.

They possess a general authority to regulate trade with foreign countries. This is a mean which has been practiced to that end, by all the principal commercial nations, who have trading companies to this day, which have subsisted for centuries. Why may not the United States, *constitutionally*, employ the means usual in other countries, for attaining the ends intrusted to them?

A power to make all needful rules and regulations concerning territory, has been construed to mean a power to erect a government. A power to regulate trade, is a power to make all needful rules and regulations concerning trade. Why may it not, then, include that of erecting a trading company, as well as, in other cases, to erect a government?

It is remarkable that the state conventions, who had proposed amendments in relation to this point, have most, if not all of them, expressed themselves nearly thus: Congress shall not grant monopolies, nor *erect any company* with exclusive advantages of commerce! Thus, at the same time, expressing their sense, that the power to erect trading companies or corporations was inherent in Congress, and objecting to it no further than as to the grant of *exclusive* privileges.

The Secretary entertains all the doubts which prevail concerning the utility of such companies, but he cannot fashion to his own mind a reason, to induce a doubt, that there is a constitutional authority in the United States to establish them. If such a reason were demanded, none could be given, unless it were this: That Congress cannot erect a corporation. Which would be no better than to say, they cannot do it, because they cannot do it— first presuming an inability, without reason, and then assigning that inability as the cause of itself.

Illustrations of this kind might be multiplied without end. They shall, however, be pursued no further.

There is a sort of evidence on this point, arising from an aggregate view of the Constitution, which is of no inconsiderable weight: the very general power of laying and collecting taxes, and appropriating their proceeds—that of borrowing money indefinitely—that of coining money, and regulating foreign coins—that of making all needful rules and regulations respecting the property of the United States. These powers combined, as well as the reason and nature of the thing, speak strongly this language: that it is the manifest design and scope of the Constitution to vest in Congress all the powers requisite to the effectual administration of the finances of the United States. As far as concerns this object, there appears to be no parsimony of power.

To suppose, then, that the government is precluded from the employment of so usual and so important an instrument for the administration of its finances as that of a bank, is to suppose what does not coincide with the general tenor and complexion of the constitution, and what is not agreeable to impressions that any new spectator would entertain concerning it. Little less than a prohibitory clause can destroy the strong presumptions which result from the general aspect of the government. Nothing but demonstration should exclude the idea that the power exists.

To all questions of this nature, the practice of mankind ought to have great weight against the theories of individuals.

The fact, for instance, that all the principal commercial nations have made use of trading corporations or companies, for the purpose of *external commerce*, is a satisfactory proof that the establishment of them is an incident to the regulation of the commerce.

This other fact, that banks are an usual engine in the administration of national finances, and an ordinary and the most effectual instrument of loan, and one which, in this country, has been found essential, pleads strongly against the supposition that a government, clothed with most of the most important prerogatives of sovereignty in relation to its revenues, its debts, its credits, its defense, its trade, its intercourse with foreign nations, is forbidden to make use of that instrument as an appendage to its own authority.

It has been stated as an auxiliary test of constitutional authority, to try whether it abridges any pre-existing right of any state, or any individual. The proposed investigation will stand the most severe examination on this point. Each state may still erect as many banks as it pleases. Every individual may still carry on the banking business to any extent he pleases.

Another criterion may be this. Whether the institution or thing has a more direct relation, as to its uses—to the objects of the reserved powers of the state governments, than to those of the powers delegated by the United States. This, rule, indeed, is less precise than the former, but it may still serve as some guide. Surely a bank has more reference to the objects intrusted to the national government than to those left to the care of the state governments. The common defense is decisive in this comparison.

It is presumed that nothing of consequence in the observations of the Secretary of State, and Attorney General, has been left unnoticed.

There are, indeed, a variety of observations of the Secretary of State designed to show that the utilities ascribed to a bank, in relation to the collection of taxes, and to trade, could be obtained without it; to analyze which, would prolong the discussion beyond all bounds. It shall be forborne for two reasons; first, because the report concerning the bank, may speak for itself in this respect; and secondly, because all those observations are grounded on the erroneous idea that the *quantum* of necessity or utility is the test of a constitutional exercise of power.

One or two remarks only shall be made. One is, that he has taken no notice of a *very essential* advantage to trade in general which is mentioned in the report, as peculiar to the existence of a bank circulation, equal in the public estimation to gold and silver. It is this that renders it unnecessary to lock up the money of the country, to accumulate for months successively, in order to the periodical payment of interest. The other is this: that his arguments to show that treasury-orders and bills of exchange, from the course of trade, will prevent any considerable displacement of the metals, are founded on a particular view of the subject. A case will prove this. The sums collected in a state may be small in comparison with the debt due to it; the balance of its trade direct and circuitous with the seat of government, may be even, or nearly so; here, then, without bank bills, which in that state answer the purpose of coin, there must be a displacement of the coin, in proportion to the difference between the sum collected in the state, and that to be paid in it. With bank bills, no such displacement would take place, or as far as it did, it would be gradual and insensible. In many other ways, also, would there be at least a temporary and inconvenient displacement of the coin, even where the course of trade would eventually return it to its proper channel.

The difference of the two situations in point of convenience to the treasury, can only be appreciated by one, who experiences the embarrassments of making provision for the payment of the interest on a stock, continually changing place in thirteen different places.

One thing which has been omitted, just occurs, although it is not very material to the main argument. The Secretary of State affirms that the bill only contemplates a repayment, not a loan, to the government. But here he is certainly mistaken. It is true the government invests in the stock of the bank a sum equal to that which it receives on loan. But let it be remembered, that it does not, therefore, cease to be a proprietor of the stock, which would be the case, if the money received back were in the nature of a payment. It remains a proprietor still, and will share in the profit or loss of the institution, according as the dividend is more or less than the interest it is to pay on the sum borrowed. Hence that sum is manifestly, and in the strictest sense, a loan.

Alexander Hamilton
Secretary of the Treasury

Report on the Subject of Manufactures

December 1791

To the Speaker of the House of Representatives:

The Secretary of the Treasury in obedience to the order of the House of Representatives, of the 15th day of January 1790, has applied his attention, at as early a period as his other duties would permit, to the subject of Manufactures; and particularly to the means of promoting such as will tend to render the United States, independent on foreign nations, for military and other essential supplies. And he thereupon respectfully submits the following Report.

The expediency of encouraging manufactures in the United States, which was not long since deemed very questionable, appears at this time to be pretty generally admitted. The embarrassments, which have obstructed the progress of our external trade, have led to serious reflections on the necessity of enlarging the sphere of our domestic commerce: the restrictive regulations, which in foreign markets abridge the vent of the increasing surplus of our Agricultural produce, serve to beget an earnest desire, that a more extensive demand for that surplus may be created at home: And the complete success, which has rewarded manufacturing enterprise, in some valuable branches, conspiring with the promising symptoms, which attend some less mature essays, in others, justify a hope, that the obstacles to the growth of this species of industry are less formidable than they were apprehended to be; and that it is not difficult to find, in its further extension; a full indemnification for any external disadvantages, which are or may be experienced, as well as an accession of resources, favorable to national independence and safety.

There still are, nevertheless, respectable patrons of opinions, unfriendly to the encouragement of manufactures. The following are, substantially, the arguments by which these opinions are defended.

"In every country (say those who entertain them) Agriculture is the most beneficial and *productive* object of human industry. This position, generally, if not universally true, applies with peculiar emphasis to the United States, on account of their immense tracts of fertile territory, uninhabited and unimproved. Nothing can afford so advantageous an employment for capital and labor, as the conversion of this extensive wilderness into cultivated farms. Nothing equally with this, can contribute to the population, strength and real riches of the country."

"To endeavor by the extraordinary patronage of Government, to accelerate the growth of manufactures, is in fact, to endeavor, by force and art, to transfer the natural current of industry, from a more to a less beneficial channel. Whatever has such a tendency must necessarily be unwise. Indeed it can hardly ever be wise in a government, to attempt to give a direction to the industry of its citizens. This under the quicksighted guidance of private interest, will, if left to itself, infallibly find its own way to the most profitable employment: and 'tis by such employment, that the public prosperity will be most effectually promoted. To leave industry to itself, therefore, is, in almost every case, the soundest as well as the simplest policy."

"This policy is not only recommended to the United States, by considerations which affect all nations, it is, in a manner, dictated to them by the imperious force of a very peculiar situation.

The smallness of their population compared with their territory—the constant allurements to emigration from the settled to the unsettled parts of the country—the facility, with which the less independent condition of an artisan can be exchanged for the more independent condition of a farmer, these and similar causes conspire to produce, and for a length of time must continue to occasion, a scarcity of hands for manufacturing occupation, and dearness of labor generally. To these disadvantages for the prosecution of manufactures, a deficiency of pecuniary capital being added, the prospect of a successful competition with the manufactures of Europe must be regarded as little less than desperate. Extensive manufactures can only be the offspring of a redundant, at least of a full population. Till the latter shall characterize the situation of this country, 'tis vain to hope for the former."

"If contrary to the natural course of things, an unseasonable and premature spring can be given to certain fabrics, by heavy duties, prohibitions, bounties, or by other forced expedients; this will only be to sacrifice the interests of the community to those of particular classes. Besides the misdirection of labor, a virtual monopoly will be given to the persons employed on such fabrics; and an enhancement of price, the inevitable consequence of every monopoly, must be defrayed at the expense of the other parts of society. It is far preferable, that those persons should be engaged in the cultivation of the earth, and that we should procure, in exchange for its productions, the commodities, with which foreigners are able to supply us in greater perfection, and upon better terms."

This mode of reasoning is founded upon facts and principles, which have certainly respectable pretensions. If it had governed the conduct of nations, more generally than it has done, there is room to suppose, that it might have carried them faster to prosperity and greatness, than they have attained, by the pursuit of maxims too widely opposite. Most general theories, however, admit of numerous exceptions, and there are few, if any, of the political kind, which do not blend a considerable portion of error, with the truths they inculcate.

In order to an accurate judgement how far that which has been just stated ought to be deemed liable to a similar imputation, it is necessary to advert carefully to the considerations, which plead in favor of manufactures, and which appear to recommend the special and positive encouragement of them; in certain cases, and under certain reasonable limitations.

It ought readily to be conceded, that the cultivation of the earth—as the primary and most certain source of national supply—as the immediate and chief source of subsistence to man—as the principal source of those materials which constitute the nutriment of other kinds of labor—as including a state most favorable to the freedom and independence of the human mind—one, perhaps, most conducive to the multiplication of the human species—has *intrinsically a strong claim to preeminence over every other kind of industry.*

But, that it has a title to anything like an exclusive predilection, in any country, ought to be admitted with great caution. That it is even more productive than every other branch of Industry requires more evidence, than has yet been given in support of the position. That its real interests, precious and important as without the help of exaggeration, they truly are, will be advanced, rather than injured by the due encouragement of manufactures, may, it is believed, be satisfactorily demonstrated. And it is also believed that the expediency of such encouragement in a general view may be shown to be recommended by the most cogent and persuasive motives of national policy.

It has been maintained, that Agriculture is, not only, the most productive, but the only productive species of industry. The reality of this suggestion in either aspect, has, however, not been verified by any accurate detail of facts and calculations; and the general arguments, which are adduced to prove it, are rather subtle and paradoxical, than solid or convincing.

Those which maintain its exclusive productiveness are to this effect.

Labor, bestowed upon the cultivation of land produces enough, not only to replace all the necessary expenses incurred in the business, and to maintain the persons who are employed in it, but to afford together with the *ordinary profit* on the stock or capital of the Farmer, a net surplus, or *rent* for the landlord or proprietor of the soil. But the labor of Artificers does nothing more, than replace the Stock which employs them (or which furnishes materials tools and wages) and yield the *ordinary profit* upon that Stock. It yields nothing equivalent to the *rent* of land. Neither does it add anything to the *total value* of the *whole annual produce* of the land and labor of the country. The additional value given to those parts of the produce of land, which are wrought into manufactures, is counterbalanced by the value of those other parts of that produce, which are consumed by the manufacturers. It can therefore only be by saving, or *parsimony* not by the positive *productiveness* of their labor, that the classes of Artificers can in any degree augment the revenue of the Society.

To this it has been answered—

I. "That inasmuch as it is acknowledged, that manufacturing labor reproduces a value equal to that which is expended or consumed in carrying it on, and continues in existence the original Stock or capital employed—it ought on that account alone, to escape being considered as wholly unproductive: That though it should be admitted, as alleged, that the consumption of the produce of the soil, by the classes of Artificers or Manufacturers, is exactly equal to the value added by their labor to the materials upon which it is exerted; yet it would not thence follow, that it added nothing to the Revenue of the Society, or to the aggregate value of the annual produce of its land and labor. If the consumption for any given period amounted to a *given sum* and the *increased* value of the produce manufactured, in the same period, to a *like sum*, the total amount of the consumption and production during that period, would be equal to the two sums, and consequently double the value of the agricultural produce consumed. And though the increment of value produced by the classes of Artificers should at no time exceed the value of the produce of the land consumed by them, yet there would be at every moment, in consequence of their labor, a greater value of goods in the market than would exist independent of it."

II. "That the position, that Artificers can augment the revenue of a Society, only by parsimony, is true in no other sense, than in one, which is equally applicable to Husbandmen or Cultivators. It may be alike affirmed of all these classes, that the fund acquired by their labor and destined for their support is not, in an ordinary way, more than equal to it. And hence it will follow, that augmentations of the wealth or capital of the community (except in the instances of some extraordinary dexterity or skill) can only proceed, with respect to any of them, from the savings of the more thrifty and parsimonious."

III. "That the annual produce of the land and labor of a country can only be increased, in two ways—by some improvement in the *productive powers* of the useful labor, which actually exists within it, or by some increase in the quantity of such labor: That with regard to the first, the labor of Artificers being capable of greater subdivision and simplicity of operation, than that of Cultivators, it is susceptible, in a proportionably greater degree, of improvement in its *productive powers*, whether to be derived from an accession of Skill, or from the application of ingenious machinery; in which particular, therefore, the labor employed in the culture of land can pretend to no advantage over that engaged in manufactures: That with regard to an augmentation of the quantity of useful labor, this, excluding adventitious circumstances, must depend essentially upon an increase of *capital*, which again must depend upon the savings made out of the revenues of those, who furnish or manage *that*, which is at any time employed, whether in Agriculture, or in Manufactures, or in any other way."

But while the *exclusive* productiveness of Agricultural labor has been thus denied and refuted, the superiority of its productiveness has been conceded without hesitation. As this concession involves a point of considerable magnitude, in relation to maxims of public administration, the grounds on which it rests are worthy of a distinct and particular examination.

One of the arguments made use of, in support of the idea may be pronounced both quaint and superficial. It amounts to this—That in the productions of the soil, nature co-operates with man; and that the effect of their joint labor must be greater than that of the labor of man alone.

This however, is far from being a necessary inference. It is very conceivable, that the labor of man alone laid out upon a work, requiring great skill and art to bring it to perfection, may be more productive, *in value*, than the labor of nature and man combined, when directed towards more simple operations and objects: And when it is recollected to what an extent the Agency of nature, in the application of the mechanical powers, is made auxiliary to the prosecution of manufactures, the suggestion, which has been noticed, loses even the appearance of plausibility.

It might also be observed, with a contrary view, that the labor employed in Agriculture is in a great measure periodical and occasional, depending on seasons, liable to various and long intermissions; while that occupied in many manufactures is constant and regular, extending through the year, embracing in some instances night as well as day. It is also probable, that there are among the cultivators of land more examples of remissness, than among artificers. The farmer, from the peculiar fertility of his land, or some other favorable circumstance, may frequently obtain a livelihood, even with a considerable degree of carelessness in the mode of cultivation; but the artisan can with difficulty effect the same object, without exerting himself pretty equally with all those, who are engaged in the same pursuit. And if it may likewise be assumed as a fact, that manufactures open a wider field to exertions of ingenuity than agriculture, it would not be a strained conjecture, that the labor employed in the former, being at once more constant, more uniform and more ingenious, than that which is employed in the latter, will be found at the same time more productive.

But it is not meant to lay stress on observations of this nature they ought only to serve as a counterbalance to those of a similar complexion. Circumstances so vague and general, as well as so abstract, can afford little instruction in a matter of this kind.

Another, and that which seems to be the principal argument offered for the superior productiveness of Agricultural labor, turns upon the allegation, that labor employed in manufactures yields nothing equivalent to the rent of land; or to that net surplus, as it is called, which accrues to the proprietor of the soil.

But this distinction, important as it has been deemed, appears rather *verbal* than *substantial.*

It is easily discernible, that what in the first instance is divided into two parts under the denominations of the *ordinary profit* of the Stock of the farmer and *rent* to the landlord, is in the second instance united under the general appellation of the *ordinary profit* on the Stock of the Undertaker; and that this formal or verbal distribution constitutes the whole difference in the two cases. It seems to have been overlooked, that the land is itself a Stock or capital, advanced or lent by its owner to the occupier or tenant, and that the rent he receives is only the ordinary profit of a certain Stock in land, not managed by the proprietor himself, but by another to whom he lends or lets it, and who on his part advances a second capital to stock and improve the land, upon which he also receives the usual profit. The rent of the landlord and the profit of the farmer are therefore nothing more than the *ordinary profits* of *two* capitals belonging to two different persons, and united in the cultivation of a farm: As in the other case, the surplus which arises upon any manufactory, after replacing the expenses of carrying it on, answers to the profits of *one* or *more* capitals engaged in the prosecution of such manufactory. It is said *one* or *more* capitals; because in fact, the same thing which is contemplated, in the case of the farm, sometimes happens in that of a manufactory. There is one, who furnishes a part of the capital, or lends a part of the money, by which it is carried on, and another, who carries it on, with the addition of his own capital. Out of the surplus, which remains, after defraying expenses, an interest is paid to the money lender for the portion of the capital furnished by him which exactly agrees with the rent paid to the landlord; and the residue of that surplus constitutes the profit of the undertaker or manufacturer, and agrees with what is denominated the ordinary profits on the Stock of the farmer. Both together make the ordinary profits of two capitals employed in a manufactory; as in the other case the rent of the landlord and the revenue of the farmer compose the ordinary profits of two Capitals employed in the cultivation of a farm.

The rent therefore accruing to the proprietor of the land, far from being a criterion of exclusive productiveness, as has been argued, is no criterion even of superior productiveness. The question must still be, whether the surplus, after defraying expenses, of a *given capital*, employed in the *purchase* and *improvement* of a piece of land, is greater or less, than that of a like capital employed in the prosecution of a manufactory: or whether the *whole value produced* from a *given capital* and a *given quantity of labor*, employed in one way, be greater or less, than the *whole value produced* from an *equal capital* and an *equal quantity of labor* employed in the other way: or rather, perhaps whether the business of Agriculture or that of Manufactures will yield the greatest product, according to a *compound ratio* of the quantity of the Capital and the quantity of labor, which are employed in the one or in the other.

The solution of either of these questions is not easy; it involves numerous and complicated details, depending on an accurate knowledge of the objects to be compared. It is not known that the comparison has ever yet been made upon sufficient data properly ascertained and analyzed. To be able to make it on the present occasion with satisfactory precision would demand more previous enquiry and investigation, than there has been hitherto either leisure or opportunity to accomplish.

Some essays however have been made towards acquiring the

requisite information; which have rather served to throw doubt upon, than to confirm the Hypothesis, under examination: But it ought to be acknowledged, that they have been too little diversified, and are too imperfect, to authorize a definitive conclusion either way; leading rather to probable conjecture than to certain deduction. They render it probable, that there are various branches of manufactures, in which a given Capital will yield a greater *total* product, and a considerably greater *net* product, than an equal capital invested in the purchase and improvement of lands; and that there are also *some* branches, in which both the *gross* and *net* produce will exceed that of Agricultural industry; according to a compound ratio of capital and labor: But it is on this last point, that there appears to be the greatest room for doubt. It is far less difficult to infer generally, that the *net produce* of Capital engaged in manufacturing enterprises is greater than that of Capital engaged in Agriculture.

In stating these results, the purchase and improvement of lands, under previous cultivation are alone contemplated. The comparison is more in favor of Agriculture, when it is made with reference to the settlement of new and waste lands; but an argument drawn from so temporary a circumstance could have no weight in determining the general question concerning the permanent relative productiveness of the two species of industry. How far it ought to influence the policy of the United States, on the score of particular situation, will be adverted to in another place.

The foregoing suggestions are *not designed to inculcate an opinion that manufacturing industry is more productive than that of Agriculture.* They are intended rather to shew that the reverse of this proposition is not ascertained; that the general arguments which are brought to establish it are not satisfactory; and consequently that a supposition of the superior productiveness of Tillage ought to be no obstacle to listening to any substantial inducements to the encouragement of manufactures, which may be otherwise perceived to exist, through an apprehension, that they may have a tendency to divert labor from a more to a less profitable employment.

It is extremely probable, that on a full and accurate development of the matter, on the ground of fact and calculation, it would be discovered that there is no material difference between the aggregate productiveness of the one, and of the other kind of industry; and that the propriety of the encouragements, which may in any case be proposed to be given to either ought to be determined upon considerations irrelative to any comparison of that nature.

II. But without contending for the superior productiveness of Manufacturing Industry, it may conduce to a better judgment of the policy, which ought to be pursued respecting its encouragement, to contemplate the subject, under some additional aspects, tending not only to confirm the idea, that this kind of industry has been improperly represented as unproductive in itself; but to evince in addition that the establishment and diffusion of manufactures have the effect of rendering the total mass of useful and productive labor in a community, *greater than it would otherwise be*. In prosecuting this discussion, it may be necessary briefly to resume and review some of the topics, which have been already touched.

To affirm, that the labor of the Manufacturer is unproductive, because he consumes as much of the produce of land, as he adds value to the raw materials which he manufactures, is not better founded, than it would be to affirm, that the labor of the farmer, which furnishes materials to the manufacturer, is unproductive, *because he consumes an equal value of manufactured articles*. Each furnishes a certain portion of the produce of his labor to the other, and each destroys a correspondent portion of the produce of the labor of the other. In the meantime, the maintenance of two Citizens, instead of one, is going on; the state has two members instead of one; and they together consume twice the value of what is produced from the land.

If instead of a farmer and artificer, there were a farmer only, he would be under the necessity of devoting a part of his labor to the fabrication of clothing and other articles, which he would procure of the artificer, in the case of there being such a person; and of course he would be able to devote less labor to the cultivation of his farm; and would draw from it a proportionably less product. The whole quantity of production, in this state of things, in provisions, raw materials and manufactures, would certainly not exceed in value the amount of what would be produced in provisions and raw materials only, if there were an artificer as well as a farmer.

Again—if there were both an artificer and a farmer, the latter would be left at liberty to pursue exclusively the cultivation of his farm. A greater quantity of provisions and raw materials would · of course be produced—equal at least—as has been already observed, to the whole amount of the provisions, raw materials and manufactures, which would exist on a contrary supposition. The artificer, at the same time would be going on in the production of manufactured commodities; to an amount sufficient not only to repay the farmer, in those commodities, for the provisions and materials which were procured from him, but to furnish the Artificer himself with a supply of similar commodities for his own use. Thus then, there would be two quantities or values in existence, instead of one; and the revenue and consumption would be double in one case, what it would be in the other.

If in place of both these suppositions, there were supposed to be two farmers, and no artificer, each of whom applied a part of his labor to the culture of land, and another part to the fabrication of Manufactures—in this case, the portion of the labor of both bestowed upon land would produce the same quantity of provisions and raw materials only, as would be produced by the entire sum of the labor of one applied in the same manner, and the portion of the labor of both bestowed upon manufactures, would produce the same quantity of manufactures only, as would be produced by the entire sum of the labor of one applied in the same manner. Hence the produce of the labor of the two farmers would not be greater than the produce of the labor of the farmer and artificer; and hence, it results, that the labor of the artificer is as positively productive as that of the farmer, and, as positively, augments the revenue of the Society.

The labor of the Artificer replaces to the farmer that portion of his labor, with which he provides the materials of exchange with the Artificer, and which he would otherwise have been compelled to apply to manufactures: and while the Artificer thus enables the farmer to enlarge his stock of Agricultural industry, a portion of which he purchases for his own use, *he also supplies himself with the manufactured articles of which he stands in need.*

He does still more—Besides this equivalent which he gives for the portion of Agricultural labor consumed by him, and this supply of manufactured commodities for his own consumption—he furnishes still a surplus, which compensates for the use of the Capital advanced either by himself or some other person, for carrying on the business. This is the ordinary profit of the stock employed in the manufactory, and is, in every sense, as effective an addition to the income of the Society, as the rent of land.

The produce of the labor of the Artificer consequently, may be regarded as composed of three parts; one by which the provisions for his subsistence and the materials for his work are purchased of the farmer, one by which he supplies himself with manufactured necessaries, and a third which constitutes the profit on the Stock employed. The two last portions seem to have been overlooked in the system, which represents manufacturing industry as barren and unproductive.

In the course of the preceding illustrations, the products of equal quantities of the labor of the farmer and artificer have been treated as if equal to each other. But this is not to be understood as intending to assert any such precise equality. It is merely a manner of expression adopted for the sake of simplicity and perspicuity. Whether the value of the produce of the labor of the farmer be somewhat more or less, than that of the artificer, is not material to the main scope of the argument, which hitherto has only aimed at shewing, that the one, as well as the other, occasions a positive augmentation of the total produce and revenue of the Society.

It is now proper to proceed a step further, and to enumerate the principal circumstances, from which it may be inferred— That manufacturing establishments not only occasion a positive augmentation of the Produce and Revenue of the Society, but that they contribute essentially to rendering them greater than they could possibly be, without such establishments. These circumstances are—

1. The division of Labor.

2. An extension of the use of Machinery.

3. Additional employment to classes of the community not-ordinarily engaged in the business.

4. The promoting of emigration from foreign Countries.

5. The furnishing greater scope for the diversity of talents and dispositions which discriminate men from each other.

6. The affording a more ample and various field for enterprise.

7. The creating in some instances a new, and securing in all, a more certain and steady demand for the surplus produce of the soil.

Each of these circumstances has a considerable influence upon the total mass of industrious effort in a community. Together, they add to it a degree of energy and effect, which are not easily conceived. Some comments upon each of them, in the order in which they have been stated, may serve to explain their importance.

I. As to the Division of Labor.

It has justly been observed, that there is scarcely any thing of greater moment in the economy of a nation, than the proper division of labor. The separation of occupations causes each to be carried to a much greater perfection, than it could possible acquire, if they were blended. This arises principally from three circumstances.

First. The greater skill and dexterity naturally resulting from a constant and undivided application to a single object. It is evident, that these properties must increase, in proportion to the separation and simplification of objects and the steadiness of the attention devoted to each; and must be less, in proportion to the complication of objects, and the number among which the attention is distracted.

Second. The economy of time—by avoiding the loss of it, incident to a frequent transition from one operation to another of a different nature. This depends on various circumstances—the transition itself—the orderly disposition of the implements, machines and materials employed in the operation to be relinquished—the preparatory steps to the commencement of a new one—the interruption of the impulse, which the mind of the workman acquires, from being engaged in a particular operation—the distractions, hesitations and reluctances, which attend the passage from one kind of business to another.

Third. An extension of the use of Machinery. A man occupied on a single object will have it more in his power, and will be more naturally led to exert his imagination in devising methods to facilitate and abridge labor, than if he were perplexed by a variety of independent and dissimilar operations. Besides this, the fabrication of Machines, in numerous instances, becoming itself a distinct trade, the Artist who follows it, has all the advantages which have been enumerated, for improvement in his particular art; and in both ways the invention and application of machinery are extended.

And from these causes united, the mere separation of the occupation of the cultivator, from that of the Artificer, has the effect of augmenting the *productive powers* of labor, and with them, the total mass of the produce or revenue of a Country. In this single view of the subject, therefore, the utility of Artificers or Manufacturers, towards promoting an increase of productive industry, is apparent.

II. As to an extension of the use of Machinery, a point which, though partly anticipated requires to be placed in one or two additional lights.

The employment of Machinery forms an item of great importance in the general mass of national industry. 'Tis an artificial force brought in aid of the natural force of man; and, to all the purposes of labor, is an increase of hands; an accession of strength, *unencumbered too by the expense of maintaining the laborer.* May it not therefore be fairly inferred, that those occupations, which give greatest scope to the use of this auxiliary, contribute most to the general Stock of industrious effort, and, in consequence, to the general product of industry?

It shall be taken for granted, and the truth of the position referred to observation, that manufacturing pursuits are susceptible in a greater degree of the application of machinery, than those of Agriculture. If so all the difference is lost to a community, which, instead of manufacturing for itself, procures the fabrics requisite to its supply from other Countries. The substitution of foreign for domestic manufactures is a transfer to foreign nations of the advantages accruing from the employment of Machinery, in the modes in which it is capable of being employed; with most utility and to the greatest extent.

The Cotton Mill invented in England, within the last twenty years, is a signal illustration of the general proposition, which has been just advanced. In consequence of it, all the different processes for spinning Cotton are performed by means of Machines, which are put in motion by water, and attended chiefly by women and Children; and by a smaller number of persons, in the whole, than are requisite in the ordinary mode of spinning. And it is an advantage of great moment that the operations of this mill continue with convenience, during the night, as well as through the day. The prodigious effect of such a Machine is easily conceived. To this invention is to be attributed essentially the immense progress, which has been so suddenly made in Great Britain in the various fabrics of Cotton.

III. As to the additional employment of classes of the community, not ordinarily engaged in the particular business.

This is not among the least valuable of the means, by which manufacturing institutions contribute to augment the general stock of industry and production. In places where those institutions prevail, besides the persons regularly engaged in them, they afford occasional and extra employment to industrious individuals and families, who are willing to devote the leisure resulting from the intermissions of their ordinary pursuits to collateral labors, as a resource of multiplying their acquisitions or their) enjoyments. The husbandman himself experiences a new source of profit and support from the increased industry of his wife and daughters; invited and stimulated by the demands of the neighboring manufactories.

Besides this advantage of occasional employment to classes having different occupations, there is another of a nature allied to it, and of a similar tendency. This is—the employment of persons who would otherwise be idle (and in many cases a burden on the community), either from the bias of temper, habit, infirmity of body, or some other cause, indisposing, or disqualifying them for the toils of the Country. It is worthy of particular remark, that, in general, women and Children are rendered more useful and the latter more early useful by manufacturing establishments, than they would otherwise be. Of the number of persons employed in the Cotton Manufactories of Great Britain, it is computed that 4/7 nearly are women and children; of whom the greatest proportion are children and many of them of a very tender age.

And thus it appears to be one of the attributes of manufactures, and one of no small consequence, to give occasion to the exertion of a greater quantity of Industry, even by the *same number* of persons, where they happen to prevail, than would exist, if there were no such establishments.

IV. As to the promoting of emigration from foreign Countries.

Men reluctantly quit one course of occupation and livelihood for another, unless invited to it by very apparent and proximate advantages. Many, who would go from one country to another, if they had a prospect of continuing with more benefit the callings, to which they have been educated, will often not be tempted to change their situation, by the hope of doing better, in some other way. Manufacturers, who listening to the powerful invitations of a better price for their fabrics, or their labor, of greater cheapness of provisions and raw materials, of an exemption from the chief part of the taxes, burdens and restraints, which they endure in the old world, of greater personal independence and consequence, under the operation of a more equal government, and of what is far more precious than mere religious toleration—a perfect equality of religious privileges; would probably flock from Europe to the United States to pursue their own trades or professions, if they were once made sensible of the advantages they would enjoy, and were inspired with an assurance of encouragement and employment, will, with difficulty, be induced to transplant themselves, with a view to becoming Cultivators of Land.

If it be true then, that it is the interest of the United States to open every possible avenue to emigration from abroad, it affords a weighty argument for the encouragement of manufactures; which for the reasons just assigned, will have the strongest tendency to multiply the inducements to it.

Here is perceived an important resource, not only for extending the population, and with it the useful and productive labor of the country, but likewise for the prosecution of manufactures, without deducting from the number of hands, which might otherwise be drawn to tillage; and even for the indemnification of Agriculture for such as might happen to be diverted from it. Many, whom Manufacturing views would induce to emigrate, would afterwards yield to the temptations, which the particular situation of this Country holds out to Agricultural pursuits. And while Agriculture would in other respects derive many signal and unmingled advantages, from the growth of manufactures, it is a problem whether it would gain or lose, as to the article of the number of persons employed in carrying it on.

V. As to the furnishing greater scope for the diversity of talents and dispositions, which discriminate men from each other.

This is a much more powerful means of augmenting the fund of national Industry than may at first sight appear. It is a just observation, that minds of the strongest and most active powers for their proper objects fall below mediocrity and labor without effect, if confined to uncongenial pursuits. And it is thence to be inferred, that the results of human exertion may be immensely increased by diversifying its objects. When all the different kinds of industry obtain in a community, each individual can find his proper element, and can call into activity the whole vigor of his nature. And the community is benefitted by the services of its respective members, in the manner, in which each can serve it with most effect.

If there be anything in a remark often to be met with— namely that there is, in the genius of the people of this country, a peculiar aptitude for mechanic improvements, it would operate as a forcible reason for giving opportunities to the exercise of that species of talent, by the propagation of manufactures.

VI. As to the affording a more ample and various field for enterprise.

This also is of greater consequence in the general scale of national exertion, than might perhaps on a superficial view be supposed, and has effects not altogether dissimilar from those of the circumstance last noticed. To cherish and stimulate the activity of the human mind, by multiplying the objects of enterprise, is not among the least considerable of the expedients, by which the wealth of a nation may be promoted. Even things in themselves not positively advantageous, sometimes become so, by their tendency to provoke exertion. Every new scene, which is opened to the busy nature of man to rouse and exert itself, is the addition of a new energy to the general stock of effort.

The spirit of enterprise, useful and prolific as it is, must necessarily be contracted or expanded in proportion to the simplicity or variety of the occupations and productions, which are to be found in a Society. It must be less in a nation of mere cultivators, than in a nation of cultivators and merchants; less in a nation of cultivators and merchants, than in a nation of cultivators, artificers and merchants.

VII. As to the creating, in some instances, a new, and securing in all a more certain and steady demand, for the surplus produce of the soil.

This is among the most important of the circumstances which have been indicated. It is a principal mean, by which the establishment of manufactures contributes to an augmentation of the produce or revenue of a country, and has an immediate and direct relation to the prosperity of Agriculture.

It is evident, that the exertions of the husbandman will be steady or fluctuating, vigorous or feeble, in proportion to the steadiness or fluctuation, adequateness, or inadequateness of the markets on which he must depend, for the vent of the surplus, which may be produced by his labor; and that such surplus in the ordinary course of things will be greater or less in the same proportion.

For the purpose of this vent, a domestic market is greatly to be preferred to a foreign one; because it is in the nature of things, far more to be relied upon.

It is a primary object of the policy of nations, to be able to supply themselves with subsistence from their own soils; and manufacturing nations, as far as circumstances permit, endeavor to procure, from the same source, the raw materials necessary for their own fabrics. This disposition, urged by the spirit of monopoly, is sometimes even carried to an injudicious extreme. It seems not always to be recollected, that nations, who have neither mines nor manufactures, can only obtain the manufactured articles, of which they stand in need, by an exchange of the products of their soils; and that, if those who can best furnish them with such articles are unwilling to give a due course to this exchange, they must of necessity make every possible effort to manufacture for themselves, the effect of which is that the manufacturing nations abridge the natural advantages of their situation, through an unwillingness to permit the Agricultural countries to enjoy the advantages of theirs, and sacrifice the interests of a mutually beneficial intercourse to the vain project of *selling every thing* and *buying nothing*.

But it is also a consequence of the policy, which has been noted, that the foreign demand for the products of Agricultural Countries, is, in a great degree, rather casual and occasional, than certain or constant. To what extent injurious interruptions of the demand for some of the staple commodities of the United States, may have been experienced, from that cause, must be referred to the judgment of those who are engaged in carrying on the commerce of the country; but it may be safely assumed, that such interruptions are at times very inconveniently felt, and that cases not unfrequently occur, in which markets are so confined and restricted, as to render the demand very unequal to the supply.

Independently likewise of the artificial impediments, which are created by the policy in question, there are natural causes tending to render the external demand for the surplus of Agricultural nations a precarious reliance. The differences of seasons, in the countries, which are consumers make immense differences in the produce of their own soils, in different years; and consequently in the degrees of their necessity for foreign supply. Plentiful harvests with them, especially if similar ones occur at the same time in the countries, which are the furnishers, occasion of course a glut in the markets of the latter.

Considering how fast and how much the progress of new settlements in the United States must increase the surplus produce of the soil, and weighing seriously the tendency of the system, which prevails among most of the commercial nations of Europe; whatever dependence may be placed on the force of natural circumstances to counteract the effects of an artificial policy; there appear strong reasons to regard the foreign demand for that surplus as too uncertain a reliance, and to desire a substitute for it, in an extensive domestic market.

To secure such a market, there is no other expedient, than

to promote manufacturing establishments. Manufacturers who constitute the most numerous class, after the Cultivators of land, are for that reason the principal consumers of the surplus of their labor.

This idea of an extensive domestic market for the surplus produce of the soil is of the first consequence. It is of all things, that which most effectually conduces to a flourishing state of Agriculture. If the effect of manufactories should be to detach a portion of the hands, which would otherwise be engaged in Tillage, it might possibly cause a smaller quantity of lands to be under cultivation but by their tendency to procure a more certain demand for the surplus produce of the soil, they would, at the same time, cause the lands which were in cultivation to be better improved and more productive. And while, by their influence, the condition of each individual farmer would be meliorated, the total mass of Agricultural production would probably be increased. For this must evidently depend as much, if not more, upon the degree of improvement; than upon the number of acres under culture.

It merits particular observation, that the multiplication of manufactories not only furnishes a Market for those articles, which have been accustomed to be produced in abundance, in a country; but it likewise creates a demand for such as were either unknown or produced in inconsiderable quantities. The bowels as well as the surface of the earth are ransacked for articles which were before neglected. Animals, Plants and Minerals acquire a utility and value, which were before unexplored.

The foregoing considerations seem sufficient to establish, as general propositions, That it is the interest of nations to diversify the industrious pursuits of the individuals, who compose them. That the establishment of manufactures is calculated not only to increase the general stock of useful and productive labor; but even to improve the state of Agriculture in particular; certainly to advance the interests of those who are engaged in it. There are other views, that will be hereafter taken of the subject, which, it is conceived, will serve to confirm these inferences.

Previously to a further discussion of the objections to the encouragement of manufactures which have been stated, it will be of use to see what can be said, in reference to the particular situation of the United States, against the conclusions appearing to result from what has been already offered.

It may be observed, and the idea is of no inconsiderable weight, that however true it might be, that a state, which possessing large tracts of vacant and fertile territory, was at the same time secluded from foreign commerce, would find its interest and the interest of Agriculture, in diverting a part of its population from Tillage to Manufactures; yet it will not follow, that the same is true of a state, which having such vacant and fertile territory, has at the same time ample opportunity of procuring from abroad, on good terms, all the fabrics of which it stands in need, for the supply of its inhabitants. The power of doing this at least secures the great advantage of a division of labor; leaving the farmer free to pursue exclusively the culture of his land, and enabling him to procure with its products the manufactured supplies requisite either to his wants or to his enjoyments. And though it should be true, that in settled countries, the diversification of Industry is conducive to an increase in the productive powers of labor, and to an augmentation of revenue and capital; yet it is scarcely conceivable that there can be anything of so solid and permanent advantage to an uncultivated and unpeopled country as to convert its wastes into cultivated and inhabited districts. If the Revenue, in the meantime, should be less, the Capital, in the event, must be greater.

To these observations, the following appears to be a satisfactory answer—

1. If the system of perfect liberty to industry and commerce were the prevailing system of nations—the arguments which dissuade a country in the predicament of the United States, from the zealous pursuits of manufactures would doubtless have great

force. It will not be affirmed, that they might not be permitted, with few exceptions, to serve as a rule of national conduct. In such a state of things, each country would have the full benefit of its peculiar advantages to compensate for its deficiencies or disadvantages. If one nation were in condition to supply manufactured articles on better terms than another, that other might find an abundant indemnification in a superior capacity to furnish the produce of the soil. And a free exchange, mutually beneficial, of the commodities which each was able to supply, on the best terms, might be carried on between them, supporting in full vigor the industry of each. And though the circumstances which have been mentioned and others, which will be unfolded hereafter render it probable, that nations merely Agricultural would not enjoy the same degree of opulence, in proportion to their numbers, as those which united manufactures with agriculture; yet the progressive improvement of the lands of the former might, in the end, atone for an inferior degree of opulence in the meantime: and in a case in which opposite considerations are pretty equally balanced, the option ought perhaps always to be, in favor of leaving Industry to its own direction.

But the system which has been mentioned, is far from characterizing the general policy of Nations. The prevalent one has been regulated by an opposite spirit. The consequence of it is, that the United States are to a certain extent in the situation of a country precluded from foreign Commerce. They can indeed, without difficulty obtain from abroad the manufactured supplies, of which they are in want; but they experience numerous and very injurious impediments to the emission and vent of their own commodities. Nor is this the case in reference to a single foreign nation only. The regulations of several countries, with which we have the most extensive intercourse, throw serious obstructions in the way of the principal staples of the United States.

In such a position of things, the United States cannot exchange with Europe on equal terms; and the want of reciprocity would render them the victim of a system, which should induce them to confine their views to Agriculture and refrain from Manufactures. A constant and increasing necessity, on their part, for the commodities of Europe, and only a partial and occasional demand for their own, in return, could not but expose them to a state of impoverishment, compared with the opulence to which their political and natural advantages authorize them to aspire.

Remarks of this kind are not made in the spirit of complaint. 'Tis for the nations, whose regulations are alluded to, to judge for themselves, whether, by aiming at too much they do not lose more than they gain. 'Tis for the United States to consider by what means they can render themselves least dependent, on the combinations, right or wrong of foreign policy.

It is no small consolation, that already the measures which have embarrassed our Trade, have accelerated internal improvements, which upon the whole have bettered our affairs. To diversify and extend these improvements is the surest and safest method of indemnifying ourselves for any inconveniences, which those or similar measures have a tendency to beget. If Europe will not take from us the products of our soil, upon terms consistent with our interest, the natural remedy is to contract as fast as possible our wants of her.

2. The conversion of their waste into cultivated lands is certainly a point of great moment in the political calculations of the United States. But the degree in which this may possibly be retarded by the encouragement of manufactories does not appear to countervail the powerful inducements to affording that encouragement.

An observation made in another place is of a nature to have great influence upon this question. If it cannot be denied, that the interests even of Agriculture may be advanced more by having such of the lands of a state as are occupied under good cultivation, than by having a greater quantity occupied under a much inferior cultivation, and if Manufactories, for the reasons assigned, must be admitted to have a tendency to promote a more steady and vigorous cultivation of the lands occupied than would happen without them—it will follow, that they are capable of indemnifying a country for a diminution of the progress of new settlements; and may serve to increase both the capital value and the income of its lands, even though they should abridge the number of acres under Tillage.

But it does, by no means, follow, that the progress of new settlements would be retarded by the extension of Manufactures. The desire of being an independent proprietor of land is founded on such strong principles in the human breast, that where the opportunity of becoming so is as great as it is in the United States, the proportion will be small of those, whose situations would otherwise lead to it, who would be diverted from it towards Manufactures. And it is highly probable, as already intimated, that the accessions of foreigners, who originally drawn over by manufacturing views would afterwards abandon them for Agricultural, would be more than equivalent for those of our own Citizens, who might happen to be detached from them.

The remaining objections to a particular encouragement of manufactures in the United States now require to be examined.

One of these turns on the proposition, that Industry, if left to itself, will naturally find its way to the most useful and profitable employment: whence it is inferred, that manufactures without the aid of government will grow up as soon and as fast, as the natural state of things and the interest of the community may require.

Against the solidity of this hypothesis, in the full latitude of the terms, very cogent reasons may be offered. These have relation to the strong influence of habit and the spirit of imitation— the fear of want of success in untried enterprises—the intrinsic difficulties incident to first essays towards a competition with those who have previously attained to perfection in the business to be attempted—the bounties, premiums and other artificial encouragements, with which foreign nations second the exertions of their own Citizens in the branches, in which they are to be rivalled.

Experience teaches, that men are often so much governed by what they are accustomed to see and practice, that the simplest and most obvious improvements, in the most ordinary occupations, are adopted with hesitation, reluctance and by slow gradations. The spontaneous transition to new pursuits, in a community long habituated to different ones, may be expected to be attended with proportionably greater difficulty. When former occupations ceased to yield a profit adequate to the subsistence of their followers, or when there was an absolute deficiency of employment in them, owing to the superabundance of hands, changes would ensue; but these changes would be likely to be more tardy than might consist with the interest either of individuals or of the Society. In many cases they would not happen, while a bare support could be ensured by an adherence to ancient courses; though a resort to a more profitable employment might be practicable. To produce the desirable changes, as early as may be expedient, may therefore require the incitement and patronage of government.

The apprehension of failing in new attempts is perhaps a more serious impediment. There are dispositions apt to be attracted by the mere novelty of an undertaking—but these are not always those best calculated to give it success. To this, it is of importance that the confidence of cautious sagacious capitalists both citizens and foreigners, should be excited. And to inspire this description of persons with confidence, it is essential, that they should be made to see in any project, which is new, and for that reason alone, if, for no other, precarious, the prospect of such a degree of countenance and support from government, as may be capable of overcoming the obstacles, inseparable from first experiments.

The superiority antecedently enjoyed by nations, who have preoccupied and perfected a branch of industry, constitutes a more formidable obstacle, than either of those, which have been mentioned, to the introduction of the same branch into a country, in which it did not before exist. To maintain between the recent establishments of one country and the long matured establishments of another country, a competition upon equal terms, both as to quality and price, is in most cases impracticable. The disparity in the one, or in the other, or in both, must necessarily be so considerable as to forbid a successful rivalship, without the extraordinary aid and protection of government.

But the greatest obstacle of all to the successful prosecution of a new branch of industry in a country, in which it was before unknown, consists, as far as the instances apply, in the bounties, premiums and other aids which are granted, in a variety of cases, by the nations, in which the establishments to be imitated are previously introduced. It is well known (and particular examples in the course of this report will be cited) that certain nations grant bounties on the exportation of particular commodities, to enable their own workmen to undersell and supplant all competitors, in the countries to which those commodities are sent. Hence the undertakers of a new manufacture have to contend not only with the natural disadvantages of a new undertaking, but with the gratuities and remunerations which other governments bestow. To be enabled to contend with success, it is evident, that the interference and aid of their own government are indispensable.

Combinations by those engaged in a particular branch of business in one country, to frustrate the first efforts to introduce it into another, by temporary sacrifices, recompensed perhaps by extraordinary indemnifications of the government of such country, are believed to have existed, and are not to be regarded as destitute of probability. The existence or assurance of aid from the government of the country, in which the business is to be introduced, may be essential to fortify adventurers against the dread of such combinations, to defeat their effects, if formed and to prevent their being formed, by demonstrating that they must in the end prove fruitless.

Whatever room there may be for an expectation that the industry of a people, under the direction of private interest, will upon equal terms find out the most beneficial employment for itself, there is none for a reliance, that it will struggle against the force of unequal terms, or will of itself surmount all the adventitious barriers to a successful competition, which may have been erected either by the advantages naturally acquired from practice and previous possession of the ground, or by those which may have sprung from positive regulations and an artificial policy. This general reflection might alone suffice as an answer to the objection under examination, exclusively of the weighty considerations which have been particularly urged.

The objections to the pursuit of manufactures in the United States, which next present themselves to discussion, represent an impracticability of success, arising from three causes—scarcity of hands—dearness of labor—want of capital.

The two first circumstances are to a certain extent real, and, within due limits, ought to be admitted as obstacles to the success of manufacturing enterprise in the United States. But there are various considerations, which lessen their force, and tend to afford an assurance that they are not sufficient to prevent the advantageous prosecution of many very useful and extensive manufactories.

With regard to scarcity of hands, the fact itself must be applied with no small qualification to certain parts of the United States. There are large districts, which may be considered as pretty fully peopled; and which notwithstanding a continual drain for distant settlement, are thickly interspersed with flourishing and increasing towns. If these districts have not already reached the point, at which the complaint of scarcity of hands ceases, they are not remote from it, and are approaching fast towards it: And having perhaps fewer attractions to agriculture, than some other parts of the Union, they exhibit a proportionably stronger tendency towards other kinds of industry. In these districts, may be discerned, no inconsiderable maturity for manufacturing establishments.

But there are circumstances, which have been already noticed with another view, that materially diminish everywhere the effect of a scarcity of hands. These circumstances are—the great use which can be made of women and children; on which point a very pregnant and instructive fact has been mentioned—the vast extension given by late improvements to the employment of Machines, which substituting the Agency of fire and water, has prodigiously lessened the necessity for manual labor—the employment of persons ordinarily engaged in other occupations, during the seasons, or hours of leisure; which, besides giving occasion to the exertion of a greater quantity of labor by the same number of persons, and thereby increasing the general stock of labor, as has been elsewhere remarked, may also be taken into the calculation, as a resource for obviating the scarcity of hands—lastly the attraction of foreign emigrants. Whoever inspects, with a careful eye, the composition of our towns will be made sensible to what an extent this resource may be relied upon. This exhibits a large proportion of ingenious and valuable workmen, in different arts and trades, who, by expatriating from Europe, have improved their own condition, and added to the industry and wealth of the United States. It is a natural inference from the experience, we have already had, that as soon as the United States shall present the countenance of a serious prosecution of Manufactures—as soon as foreign artists shall be made sensible that the state of things here affords a moral certainty of employment and encouragement—competent numbers of European workmen will transplant themselves, effectually to ensure the success of the design. How indeed can it otherwise happen considering the various and powerful inducements, which the situation of this country offers; addressing themselves to so many strong passions and feelings, to so many general and particular interests?

It may be affirmed therefore, in respect to hands for carrying on manufactures, that we shall in great measure trade upon a foreign Stock; reserving our own, for the cultivation of our lands and the manning of our Ships; as far as character and circumstances shall incline. It is not unworthy of remark, that the objection to the success of manufactures, deduced from the scarcity of hands, is alike applicable to Trade and Navigation; and yet these are perceived to flourish, without any sensible impediment from that cause.

As to the dearness of labor (another of the obstacles alleged) this has relation principally to two circumstances, one that which has been just discussed, or the scarcity of hands, the other, the greatness of profits.

As far as it is a consequence of the scarcity of hands, it is mitigated by all the considerations which have been adduced as lessening that deficiency.

It is certain too, that the disparity in this respect, between some of the most manufacturing parts of Europe and a large proportion of the United States, is not nearly so great as is commonly imagined. It is also much less in regard to Artificers and manufacturers than in regard to country laborers; and while a careful comparison shows, that there is, in this particular, much exaggeration; it is also evident that the effect of the degree of disparity, which does truly exist, is diminished in proportion to the use which can be made of machinery.

To illustrate this last idea—Let it be supposed, that the difference of price, in two Countries, of a given quantity of manual labor requisite to the fabrication of a given article is as 10; and that some *mechanic power* is introduced into both countries, which performing half the necessary labor, leaves only half to be done by hand, it is evident, that the difference in the cost of the fabrication of the article in question, in the two countries, as far as it is connected with the price of labor, will be reduced from 10 to 5, in consequence of the introduction of that *power*.

This circumstance is worthy of the most particular attention. It diminishes immensely one of the objections most strenuously urged, against the success of manufactures in the United States.

To procure all such machines as are known in any part of Europe, can only require a proper provision and due pains. The knowledge of several of the most important of them is already possessed. The preparation of them here, is in most cases, practicable on nearly equal terms. As far as they depend on Water, some superiority of advantages may be claimed, from the uncommon variety and greater cheapness of situations adapted to Mill seats, with which different parts of the United States abound.

So far as the dearness of labor may be a consequence of the greatness of profits in any branch of business, it is no obstacle to its success. The Undertaker can afford to pay the price.

There are grounds to conclude that undertakers of Manufacturers in this Country can at this time afford to pay higher wages to the workmen they may employ than are paid to similar workmen in Europe. The prices of foreign fabrics, in the markets of the United States, which will for a long time regulate the prices of the domestic ones, may be considered as compounded of the following ingredients—The first cost of materials, including the Taxes, if any, which are paid upon them where they are made: the expense of grounds, buildings machinery and tools: the wages of the persons employed in the manufactory: the profits on the capital or Stock employed: the commissions of Agents to purchase them where they are made; the expense of transportation to the United States, including insurance and other incidental charges; the taxes on duties, if any, and fees of office which are paid on their exportation— the taxes or duties, and fees of office which are paid on their importation.

As to the first of these items, the cost of materials, the advantage upon the whole, is at present on the side of the United States, and the difference, in their favor, must increase, in proportion as a certain and extensive domestic demand shall induce the proprietors of land to devote more of their attention to the production of those materials. It ought not to escape observation, in a comparison on this point, that some of the principal manufacturing Countries of Europe are much more dependent on foreign supply for the materials of their manufactures, than would be the United States, who are capable of supplying themselves, with a greater abundance, as well as a greater variety of the requisite materials.

As to the second item, the expense of grounds, buildings, machinery, and tools, an equality at least may be assumed; since advantages in some particulars will counterbalance temporary disadvantages in others.

As to the third item, or the article of wages, the comparison certainly turns against the United States, though as before observed not in so great a degree as is commonly supposed.

The fourth item is alike applicable to the foreign and to the domestic manufacture. It is indeed more properly a *result* than a particular, to be compared.

But with respect to all the remaining items, they are alone applicable to the foreign manufacture, and in the strictest sense extraordinaries; constituting a sum of extra charge on the foreign fabric, which cannot be estimated, at less than from 15 to 30 percent on the cost of it at the manufactory.

This sum of extra charge may confidently be regarded as more than a Counterpoise for the real difference in the price of labor; and is a satisfactory proof that manufactures may prosper in defiance of it in the United States. To the general allegation, connected with the circumstances of scarcity of hands and dearness of labor, that extensive manufactures can only grow out of a redundant or full population, it will be sufficient, to answer generally, that the fact has been otherwise—That the situation alleged to be an essential condition of success, has not been that of several nations, at periods when they had already attained to maturity in a variety of manufactures.

The supposed want of Capital for the prosecution of manufactures in the United States is the most indefinite of the objections which are usually opposed to it.

It is very difficult to pronounce anything precise concerning the real extent of the monied capital of a Country, and still more concerning the proportion which it bears to the objects that invite the employment of Capital. It is not less difficult to pronounce how far the effect of any given quantity of money, as capital, or in other words, as a medium for circulating the industry and property of a nation, may be increased by the very circumstance of the additional motion, which is given to it by new objects of employment. That effect, like the momentum of descending bodies, may not improperly be represented, as in a compound ratio to mass and velocity. It seems pretty certain, that a given sum of money, in a situation, in which the quick impulses of commercial activity were little felt, would appear inadequate to the circulation of as great a quantity of industry and property, as in one, in which their full influence was experienced.

It is not obvious, why the same objection might not as well be made to external commerce as to manufactures; since it is manifest that our immense tracts of land occupied and unoccupied are capable of giving employment to more capital than is actually bestowed upon them. It is certain, that the United States offer a vast field for the advantageous employment of Capital; but it does not follow, that there will not be found, in one way or another, a sufficient fund for the successful prosecution of any species of industry which is likely to prove truly beneficial.

The following considerations are of a nature to remove all inquietude on the score of want of Capital.

The introduction of Banks, as has been shown on another occasion, has a powerful tendency to extend the active Capital of a Country. Experience of the Utility of these Institutions is multiplying them in the United States. It is probable that they will be established wherever they can exist with advantage; and wherever, they can be supported, if administered with prudence, they will add new energies to all pecuniary operations.

The aid of foreign Capital may safely, and, with considerable latitude be taken into calculation. Its instrumentality has been long experienced in our external commerce; and it has begun to be felt in various other modes. Not only our funds, but our Agriculture and other internal improvements have been animated by it. It has already in a few instances extended even to our manufactures.

It is a well known fact, that there are parts of Europe, which have more Capital, than profitable domestic objects of employment. Hence, among other proofs, the large loans continually furnished to foreign states. And it is equally certain that the capital of other parts may find more profitable employment in the United States, than at home. And notwithstanding there are weighty inducements to prefer the employment of capital at home even at less profit, to an investment of it abroad, though with greater gain, yet these inducements are overruled either by a deficiency of employment or by a very material difference in profit. Both these Causes operate to produce a transfer of foreign capital to the United States. 'Tis certain, that various objects in this country hold out advantages, which are with difficulty to be equaled elsewhere; and under the increasingly favorable impressions, which are entertained of our government, the attractions will become more and More strong. These impressions will prove a rich mine of prosperity to the Country, if they are confirmed and strengthened by the progress of our affairs. And to secure this advantage, little more is now necessary, than to foster industry, and cultivate order and tranquility, at home and abroad.

It is not impossible, that there may be persons disposed to look with a jealous eye on the introduction of foreign Capital, as if it were an instrument to deprive our own citizens of the profits of our own industry: But perhaps there never could be a more unreasonable jealousy. Instead of being viewed as a rival, it ought to be Considered as a most valuable auxiliary; conducing to put in Motion a greater Quantity of productive labor, and a greater portion of useful enterprise than could exist without it. It is at least evident, that in a Country situated like the United States, with an infinite fund of resources yet to be unfolded, every farthing of foreign capital, which is laid out in internal ameliorations, and in industrious establishments of a permanent nature, is a precious acquisition.

And whatever be the objects which originally attract foreign Capital, when once introduced, it may be directed towards any purpose of beneficial exertion, which is desired. And to detain it among us, there can be no expedient so effectual as to enlarge the sphere, within which it may be usefully employed: Though induced merely with views to speculations in the funds, it may afterwards be rendered subservient to the Interests of Agriculture, Commerce and Manufactures.

But the attraction of foreign Capital for the direct purpose of Manufactures ought not be deemed a chimerical expectation. There are already examples of it, as remarked in another place. And the examples, if the disposition be cultivated can hardly fail to multiply. There are also instances of another kind, which serve to strengthen the expectation. Enterprises for improving the Public Communications, by cutting canals, opening the obstructions in Rivers and erecting bridges, have received very material aid from the same source.

When the Manufacturing Capitalist of Europe shall advert to the many important advantages, which have been intimated, in the Course of this report, he cannot but perceive very powerful inducements to a transfer of himself and his Capital to the United States. Among the reflections, which a most interesting peculiarity of situation is calculated to suggest, it cannot escape his observation, as a circumstance of Moment in the calculation that the progressive population and improvement of the United States insure a continually increasing domestic demand for the fabrics which he shall produce, not to be affected by any external casualties or vicissitudes.

But while there are Circumstances sufficiently strong to authorize a considerable degree of reliance on the aid of foreign Capital towards the attainment of the object in view, it999999 is satisfactory to have good grounds of assurance, that there are domestic resources of themselves adequate to it. It happens, that there is a species of Capital actually existing within the United States, which relieves from all inquietude on the score of want of Capital—This is the funded Debt.

The effect of a funded debt, as a species of Capital, has been

Noticed upon a former Occasion; but a more particular elucidation of the point seems to be required by the stress which is here laid upon it. This shall accordingly be attempted.

Public Funds answer the purpose of Capital, from the estimation in which they are usually held by Monied men; and consequently from the Ease and dispatch with which they can be turned into money. This capacity of prompt convertibility into money causes a transfer of stock to be in a great number of Cases equivalent to a payment in coin. And where it does not happen to suit the party who is to receive, to accept a transfer of Stock, the party who is to pay, is never at a loss to find elsewhere a purchaser of his Stock, who will furnish him in lieu of it, with the Coin of which he stands in need. Hence in a sound and settled state of the public funds, a man possessed of a sum in them can embrace any scheme of business, which offers, with as much confidence as if he were possessed of an equal sum in Coin.

This operation of public funds as capital is too obvious to be denied; but it is objected to the Idea of their operating as an augmentation of the Capital of the community, that they serve to occasion the destruction of some other capital to an equal amount.

The Capital which alone they can be supposed to destroy must consist of—The annual revenue, which is applied to the payment of Interest on the debt, and to the gradual redemption of the principal—The amount of the Coin, which is employed in circulating the funds, or, in other words, in effecting the different alienations which they undergo.

But the following appears to be the true and accurate view of this matter.

First. As to the point of the Annual Revenue requisite for Payment of interest and redemption of principal.

As a determinate proportion will tend to perspicuity in the reasoning, let it be supposed that the annual revenue to be applied, corresponding with the modification of the 6 percent stock of the United States, is in the ratio of eight upon the hundred, that is in the first instance six on Account of interest, and two on account of Principal.

Thus far it is evident, that the Capital destroyed to the capital created, would bear no greater proportion, than 8 to 100. There would be withdrawn from the total mass of other capitals a sum of eight dollars to be paid to the public creditor; while he would be possessed of a sum of One Hundred dollars, ready to be applied to any purpose, to be embarked in any enterprise, which might appear to him eligible. Here then the *Augmentation* of Capital, or the excess of that which is produced, beyond that which is destroyed is equal to Ninety two dollars. To this conclusion, it may be objected, that the sum of Eight dollars is to be withdrawn annually, until the whole hundred is extinguished, and it may be inferred, that in process of time a capital will be destroyed equal to that which is at first created.

But it is nevertheless true, that during the whole of the interval, between the creation of the Capital of 100 dollars, and its reduction to a sum not greater than that of the annual revenue appropriated to its redemption—there will be a greater active capital in existence than if no debt had been Contracted. The sum drawn from other Capitals *in any one year* will not exceed eight dollars; but there will be *at every instant of time* during the whole period, in question a sum corresponding *with so much of the principal,* as remains *unredeemed,* in the hands of some person, or other, employed, or ready to be employed in some profitable undertaking. There will therefore constantly be more capital, in capacity to be employed, than capital taken from employment. The excess for the first year has been stated to be Ninety two dollars; it will diminish yearly, but there always will be an excess, until the principal of the debt is brought to a level with the *redeeming annuity,* that is, in the case which has been assumed by way of example, to *eight dollars.* The reality of this excess becomes palpable, if it be supposed, as often happens, that the citizen of a foreign Country imports into the United States 100 dollars for the purchase of an equal sum of public debt. Here is an absolute augmentation of the mass of Circulating Coin to the extent of 100 dollars. At the end of a year the foreigner is presumed to draw back eight dollars on account of his Principal and Interest, but he still leaves, Ninety two of his original Deposit in circulation, as he in like manner leaves Eighty four at the end of the second year, drawing back then also the annuity of Eight Dollars: And thus the Matter proceeds; The capital left in circulation diminishing each year, and coming nearer to the level of the annuity drawn back. There are however some differences in the ultimate operation of the part of the debt, which is purchased by foreigners, and that which remains in the hands of citizens. But the general effect in each case, though in different degrees, is to add to the active capital of the Country.

Hitherto the reasoning has proceeded on a concession of the position, that there is a destruction of some other capital, to the extent of the annuity appropriated to the payment of the Interest and the redemption of the principal of the debt but in this, too much has been conceded. There is at most a temporary transfer of some other capital, to the amount of the Annuity, from those who pay to the Creditor who receives; which he again restores to the circulation to resume the offices of a capital. This he does either immediately by employing the money in some branch of Industry, or mediately by lending it to some other person, who does so employ it or by spending it on his own maintenance. In either supposition there is no destruction of capital, there is nothing more than a suspension of its motion for a time; that is, while it is passing from the hands of those who pay into the Public coffers, and thence through the public Creditor into some other Channel of circulation. When the payments of interest are periodical and quick and made by instrumentality of Banks the diversion or suspension of capital may almost be denominated momentary. Hence the deduction on this Account is far less, than it at first sight appears to be.

There is evidently, as far as regards the annuity no destruction nor transfer of any other Capital, than that portion of the income of each individual, which goes to make up the Annuity.

The land which furnishes the Farmer with the sum which he is to contribute remains the same; and the like may be observed of other Capitals. Indeed as far as the Tax, which is the object of contribution (as frequently happens, when it does not oppress, by its weight) may have been a Motive to *greater exertion* in any occupation; it may even serve to increase the contributory Capital: This idea is not without importance in the general view of the subject.

It remains to see, what further deduction ought to be made from the capital which is created, by the existence of the Debt; on account of the coin, which is employed in its circulation. This is susceptible of much less precise calculation, than the Article which has just been discussed. It is impossible to say what proportion of coin is necessary to carry on the alienations which any species of property usually undergoes. The quantity indeed varies according to circumstances. But it may still without hesitation be pronounced, from the quickness of the rotation, or rather of the transitions, that the *medium* of circulation always bears but a small proportion to the amount of the *property* circulated. And it is thence satisfactorily deducible, that the coin employed in the Negotiations of the funds and which serves to give them activity, as capital, is incomparably less than the sum of the debt negotiated for the purposes of business.

It ought not however, to be omitted, that the negotiation of the funds becomes itself a distinct business; which employs, and by employing diverts a portion of the circulating coin from other pursuits. But making due allowance for this circumstance there is no reason to conclude, that the effect of the diversion of coin in the whole operation bears any considerable proportion to the amount of the Capital to which it gives activity. The sum of the debt in circulation is continually at the Command, of any useful enterprise—the coin itself which circulates it, is never more than momentarily suspended from its ordinary functions. It experiences an incessant and rapid flux and reflux to and from the Channels of industry to those of speculations in the funds.

There are strong circumstances in confirmation of this Theory. The force of Monied Capital which has been displayed in Great Britain, and the height to which every species of industry has grown up under it, defy a solution from the quantity of coin which that kingdom has ever possessed. Accordingly it has been Coeval with its funding system, the prevailing opinion of the men of business, and of the generality of the most sagacious theorists of that country, that the operation of the public funds as capital has contributed to the effect in question. Among ourselves appearances thus far favor the same Conclusion. Industry in general seems to have been reanimated. There are symptoms indicating an extension of our Commerce. Our navigation has certainly of late had a Considerable spring, and there appears to be in many parts of the Union a command of capital, which till lately, since the revolution at least, was unknown. But it is at the same time to be acknowledged, that other circumstances have concurred, (and in a great degree) in producing the present state of things, and that the appearances are not yet sufficiently decisive, to be entirely relied upon.

In the question under discussion, it is important to distinguish between an *absolute increase of Capital, or an accession of real wealth,* and an *artificial increase of Capital,* as an engine of business, or as an instrument of industry and Commerce. In the first sense, a funded debt has no pretensions to being deemed an increase of Capital; in the last, it has pretensions which are not easy to be controverted. Of a similar nature is bank credit and in an inferior degree, every species of private credit.

But though a funded debt is not in the first instance, an absolute increase of Capital, or an augmentation of real wealth; yet by serving as a New power in the operation of industry, it has within certain bounds a tendency to increase the real wealth of a Community, in like manner as money borrowed by a thrifty farmer, to be laid out in the improvement of his farm may, in the end, add to his Stock of real riches.

There are respectable individuals, who from a just aversion

to an accumulation of Public debt, are unwilling to concede to it any kind of utility, who can discern no good to alleviate the ill with which they suppose it pregnant; who cannot be persuaded that it ought in any sense to be viewed as an increase in capital lest it should be inferred, that the more debt the more capital, the greater the burdens the greater the blessings of the community.

But it interests the public Councils to estimate every object as it truly is; to appreciate how far the good in any measure is compensated by the ill; or the ill by the good. Either of them is seldom unmixed.

Neither will it follow, that an accumulation of debt is desirable, because a certain degree of it operates as capital. There may be a plethora in the political, as in the Natural body; There may be a state of things in which any such artificial capital is unnecessary. The debt too may be swelled to such a size, as that the greatest part of it may cease to be useful as a Capital, serving only to pamper the dissipation of idle and dissolute individuals: as that the sums required to pay the Interest upon it may become oppressive, and beyond the means, which a government can employ, consistently with its tranquility, to raise them; as that the resources of taxation, to face the debt, may have been strained too far to admit of extensions adequate to exigencies, which regard the public safety.

Where this critical point is, cannot be pronounced, but it is impossible to believe, that there is not such a point.

And as the vicissitudes of Nations beget a perpetual tendency to the accumulation of debt, there ought to be in every government a perpetual, anxious and unceasing effort to reduce that, which at any time exists, as fast as shall be practicable consistently with integrity and good faith.

Reasonings on a subject comprehending ideas so abstract and complex, so little reducible to precise calculation as those which enter into the question just discussed, are always attended with a danger of running into fallacies. Due allowance ought therefore to be made for this possibility. But as far as the Nature of the subject admits of it, there appears to be satisfactory ground for a belief, that the public funds operate as a resource of capital to the Citizens of the United States, and, if they are a resource at all, it is an extensive one.

To all the arguments which are brought to evince the impracticability of success in manufacturing establishments in the United States, it might have been a sufficient answer to have referred to the experience of what has been already done. It is certain that several important branches have grown up and flourished with a rapidity which surprises: affording an encouraging assurance of success in future attempts: of these it may not be improper to enumerate the most considerable.

I. of Skins

Tanned and tawed leather dressed skins, shoes, boots and Slippers, harness and saddlery of all kinds. Portmanteaus and trunks, leather breeches, gloves, muffs and tippets, parchment and Glue.

II. of Iron

Barr and Sheet Iron, Steel, Nail-rods and Nails, implements of husbandry, Stoves, pots and other household utensils, the steel and Iron work of carriages and for Shipbuilding, Anchors, scale beams and Weights and Various tools of Artificers, arms of different kinds; though the manufacture of these last has of late diminished for want of demand.

III. of Wood

Ships, Cabinet Wares and Turnery, Wool and Cotton cards and other Machinery for manufactures and husbandry, Mathematical instruments, Cooper's wares of every kind.

IV. of Flax and Hemp

Cables, sail-cloth, Cordage, twine and pack-thread.

V. Bricks and coarse tiles and Potters Wares.

VI. Ardent Spirits and malt liquors.

VII. Writing and printing Paper, sheathing and Wrapping Paper, pasteboards, fillers or press papers, paper hangings.

VIII. Hats of fur and Wool and of mixtures of both, Women's Stuff and Silk shoes.

IX. Refined Sugars.

X. Oil of Animals and seeds; Soap, Spermaceti and Tallow Candles.

XI. Copper and brass wares, particularly utensils for distillers, Sugar refiners and brewers, And—Irons and other Articles for household Use, philosophical apparatus.

XII. Tin Wares, for most purposes of Ordinary use.

XIII. Carriages of all kinds.

XIV. Snuff, chewing and smoking Tobacco.

XV. Starch and Hairpowder.

XVI. Lampblack and other painters colors.

XVII. Gunpowder.

Besides manufactories of these articles which are carried on as regular Trades, and have attained to a considerable degree of maturity, there is a vast scene of household manufacturing, which contributes more largely to the supply of the Community, than could be imagined; without having made it an object of particular enquiry. This observation is the pleasing result of the investigation, to which the subject of the report has led, and is applicable as well to the Southern as to the middle and Northern States; great quantities of coarse cloths, coatings, serges, and flannels, linsey Woolseys, hosiery of Wool, cotton and thread, coarse fustians, jeans and Muslins, checked and striped cotton and linen goods, bed ticks, Coverlets and Counterpanes, Tow linens, coarse shirtings, sheetings, toweling and table linen, and various mixtures of wool and cotton, and of Cotton and flax are made in the household way, and in many instances to an extent not only sufficient for the supply of the families in which they are made, but for sale, and even in some casesfor exportation. It is computed in a number of districts that 2/3, 3/4 and even 4/5 of all the Clothing of the Inhabitants are made by themselves. The importance of so great a progress, as appears to have been made in family Manufactures, within a few years, both in a moral and political view, renders the fact highly interesting.

Neither does the above enumeration comprehend all the articles that are manufactured as regular Trades. Many others occur, which are equally well established, but which not being of equal importance have been omitted. And there are many attempts still in their Infancy, which though attended with very favorable appearances, could not have been properly comprised in an enumeration of manufactories already established. There are other articles also of great importance, which tho' strictly speaking manufactures are omitted, as being immediately connected with husbandry: such are flour, pot and pearl ash, Pitch, tar, turpentine and the like.

There remains to be noticed an objection to the encouragement of manufactures, of a nature different from those which question the probability of success. This is derived from its supposed tendency to give a monopoly of advantages to particular classes at the expense of the rest of the community, who, it is affirmed, would be able to procure the requisite supplies of manufactured articles on better terms from foreigners, than from our own Citizens, and who it is alleged, are reduced to a necessity of paying an enhanced price for whatever they want, by every measure, which obstructs the free competition of foreign commodities.

It is not an unreasonable supposition, that measures, which serve to abridge the free competition of foreign Articles, have a tendency to occasion an enhancement of prices and it is not to be denied that such is the effect in a number of Cases; but the fact does not uniformly correspond with the theory. A reduction of prices has in several instances immediately succeeded the establishment of a domestic manufacture. Whether it be that foreign

Manufacturers endeavor to supplant by underselling our own, or whatever else be the cause, the effect has been such as is stated, and the reverse of what might have been expected.

But though it were true, that the immediate and certain effect of regulations controlling the competition of foreign with domestic fabrics was an increase of price, it is universally true, that the contrary is the ultimate effect with every successful manufacture. When a domestic manufacture has attained to perfection, and has engaged in the prosecution of it a competent number of Persons, it invariably becomes cheaper. Being free from the heavy charges, which attend the importation of foreign commodities, it can be afforded, and accordingly seldom or never fails to be sold Cheaper, in process of time, than was the foreign Article for which it is a substitute. The internal competition, which takes place, soon does away every thing like Monopoly, and by degrees reduces the price of the Article to the minimum of a reasonable profit on the Capital employed. This accords with the reason of the thing and with experience.

Whence it follows, that it is the interest of a community with a view to eventual and permanent economy, to encourage the growth of manufactures. In a national view, a temporary enhancement of price must always be well compensated by a permanent reduction of it.

It is a reflection, which may with propriety be indulged here, that this eventual diminution of the prices of manufactured Articles, which is the result of internal manufacturing establishments, has a direct and very important tendency to benefit agriculture. It enables the farmer, to procure with a smaller quantity of his labor, the manufactured produce of which he stands in need, and consequently increases the value of his income and property.

The objections which are commonly made to the expediency of encouraging, and to the probability of succeeding in manufacturing pursuits, in the United States, having now been discussed; the Considerations which have appeared in the Course of the discussion, recommending that species of industry to the patronage of the Government, will be materially strengthened by a few general and some particular topics, which have been naturally reserved for subsequent Notice.

I. There seems to be a moral certainty, that the trade of a country which is both manufacturing and Agricultural will be more lucrative and prosperous, than that of a Country, which is merely Agricultural.

One reason for this is found in that general effort of nations (which has been already mentioned) to procure from their own soils, the articles of prime necessity requisite to their own consumption and use; and which serves to render their demand for a foreign supply of such articles in a great degree occasional and contingent. Hence, while the necessities of nations exclusively devoted to Agriculture, for the fabrics of manufacturing states, are constant and regular, the wants of the latter for the products of the former, are liable to very considerable fluctuations and interruptions. The great inequalities resulting from difference of seasons, have been elsewhere remarked: This uniformity of demand on one side, and unsteadiness of it, on the other, must necessarily have a tendency to cause the general course of the exchange of commodities between the parties to turn to the disadvantage of the merely agricultural States. Peculiarity of situation, a climate and soil adapted to the production of peculiar commodities, may, sometimes, contradict the rule; but there is every reason to believe that it will be found in the Main, a just one.

Another circumstance which gives a superiority of commercial advantage to states, that manufacture as well as cultivate, consists in the more numerous attractions, which a more diversified market offers to foreign Customers, and greater scope, which it affords to mercantile enterprise. It is a position of indisputable truth in Commerce, depending too on very obvious reasons, that the greatest resort will ever be to those marts where commodities, while equally abundant, are most various. Each difference of kind holds out an additional inducement. And it is a position not less clear, that the field of enterprise must be enlarged to the

Merchants of a Country, in proportion to the variety as well as the abundance of commodities which they find at home for exportation to foreign Markets.

A third circumstance, perhaps not inferior to either of the other two, conferring the superiority which has been stated has relation to the stagnations of demand for certain commodities which at some time or other interfere more or less with the sale of all. The nation which can bring to Market but few articles is likely to be more quickly and sensibly affected by such stagnations, than one, which is always possessed of a great variety of commodities. The former frequently finds too great a proportion of its stock of materials, for sale or exchange, lying on hand—or is obliged to make injurious sacrifices to supply its wants of foreign articles, which are *Numerous* and *urgent*, in proportion to the smallness of the number of its own. The latter commonly finds itself indemnified, by the high prices of some articles, for the low prices of others—and the Prompt and advantageous sale of those articles which are in demand enables its merchant the better to wait for a favorable change, in respect to those which are not. There is ground to believe, that a difference of situation, in this particular, has immensely different effects upon the wealth and prosperity of Nations.

From these circumstances collectively, two important inferences are to be drawn, one, that there is always a higher probability of a favorable balance of Trade, in regard to countries in which manufactures founded on the basis of a thriving Agriculture flourish, than in regard to those, which are confined wholly or almost wholly to Agriculture; the other (which is also a consequence of the first), that countries of the former description are likely to possess more pecuniary wealth, or money, than those of the latter.

Facts appear to correspond with this conclusion. The importations of manufactured supplies seem invariably to drain the merely Agricultural people of their wealth. Let the situation of the manufacturing countries of Europe be compared in this particular, with that of Countries which only cultivate, and the disparity will be striking. Other causes, it is true, help to Account for this disparity between some of them; and among these causes, the relative state of Agriculture; but between others of them, the most prominent circumstance of dissimilitude arises from the Comparative state of Manufactures. In corroboration of the same idea, it ought not to escape remark, that the West India Islands, the soils of which are the most fertile, and the Nation, which in the greatest degree supplies the rest of the world, with the precious metals, exchange to a loss with almost every other Country.

As far as experience at home may guide, it will lead to the same conclusion. Previous to the revolution, the quantity of coin, possessed by the colonies, which now compose the United states, appeared, to be inadequate to their circulation; and their debt to Great Britain was progressive. Since the Revolution, the states, in which manufactures have most increased, have recovered fastest from the injuries of the late War, and abound most in pecuniary resources.

It ought to be admitted, however in this as in the preceding case, that causes irrelative to the state of manufactures account, in a degree, for the Phenomena remarked. The continual progress of new settlements has a natural tendency to occasion an unfavorable balance of Trade; though it indemnifies for the inconvenience, by that increase of the national capital which flows from the conversion of waste into improved lands: And the different degrees of external commerce, which are carried on by the different States, may make material differences in the comparative state of their wealth. The first circumstance has reference to the deficiency of coin and the increase of debt previous to the revolution; the last to the advantages which the most manufacturing states appear to have enjoyed, over the others, since the termination of the late War.

But the uniform appearance of an abundance of specie, as the concomitant of a flourishing state of manufactures and of the reverse, where they do not prevail, afford a strong presumption of their favorable operation upon the wealth of a Country.

Not only the wealth; but the independence and security of a Country, appear to be materially connected with the prosperity of manufactures. Every nation, with a view to those great objects, ought to endeavor to possess within itself all the essentials of national supply. These comprise the means of *Subsistence, habitation, clothing,* and *defense.*

The possession of these is necessary to the perfection of the body politic, to the safety as well as to the welfare of the society; the want of either, is the want of an important organ of political life and Motion; and in the various crises which await a state, it must severely feel the effects of any such deficiency. The extreme embarrassments of the United States during the late War, from an incapacity of supplying themselves, are still matter of keen recollection: A future war might be expected again to exemplify the mischiefs and dangers of a situation, to which that incapacity is still in too great a degree applicable, unless changed by timely and vigorous exertion. To effect this change as fast as shall be prudent, merits all the attention and all the Zeal of our Public Councils; 'tis the next great work to be accomplished.

The want of a Navy to protect our external commerce, as long as it shall Continue, must render it a peculiarly precarious reliance, for the supply of essential articles, and must serve to strengthen prodigiously the arguments in favor of manufactures.

To these general Considerations are added some of a more particular nature.

Our distance from Europe, the great fountain of manufactured supply, subjects us in the existing state of things, to inconvenience and loss in two Ways.

The bulkiness of those commodities which are the chief productions of the soil, necessarily imposes very heavy charges on their transportation, to distant markets. These charges, in the Cases, in which the nations, to whom our products are sent, maintain a Competition in the supply of their own markets, principally fall upon us, and form material deductions from the primitive value of the articles furnished. The charges on manufactured supplies, brought from Europe are greatly enhanced by the same circumstance of distance. These charges, again, in the cases in which our own industry maintains no competition, in our own markets, also principally fall upon us; and are an additional cause of extraordinary deduction from the primitive value of our own products; these being the materials of exchange for the foreign fabrics, which we consume.

The equality and moderation of individual property and the growing settlements of new districts, occasion in this country an unusual demand for coarse manufactures; The charges of which being greater in proportion to their greater bulk augment the disadvantage, which has been just described.

As in most countries domestic supplies maintain a very considerable competition with such foreign productions of the soil, as are imported for sale; if the extensive establishment of Manufactories in the United States does not create a similar competition in respect to manufactured articles, it appears to be clearly deducible, from the Considerations which have been mentioned, that they must sustain a double loss in their exchanges with foreign Nations; strongly conducive to an unfavorable balance of Trade, and very prejudicial to their Interests.

These disadvantages press with no small weight, on the landed interest of the Country. In seasons of peace, they cause a serious deduction from the intrinsic value of the products of the soil. In the time of a War, which should either involve ourselves, or another nation, possessing a Considerable share of our carrying trade, the charges on the transportation of our commodities, bulky as most of them are, could hardly fail to prove a grievous burden to the farmer; while obliged to depend in so great degree as he now does, upon foreign markets for the vent of the surplus of his labor.

As far as the prosperity of the Fisheries of the United States is impeded by the want of an adequate market, there arises another special reason for desiring the extension of manufactures. Besides the fish, which in many places, would be likely to make a part of the subsistence of the persons employed; it is known that the oils, bones, and skins of marine animals, are of extensive use in various manufactures. Hence the prospect of an additional demand for the produce of the Fisheries.

One more point of view only remains in which to Consider the expediency of encouraging manufactures in the United states.

It is not uncommon to meet with an opinion that though the promoting of manufactures may be the interest of a part of the Union, it is contrary to that of another part. The Northern and southern regions are sometimes represented as having adverse interests in this respect. Those are called Manufacturing, these Agricultural states; and a species of opposition is imagined to subsist between the Manufacturing and Agricultural interests.

This idea of an opposition between those two interests is the common error of the early periods of every country, but experience gradually dissipates it. Indeed they are perceived so often to succor and to befriend each other, that they come at length to be considered as one: a supposition which has been frequently abused and is not universally true. Particular encouragements of particular manufactures may be of a Nature to sacrifice the interests of landholders to those of manufacturers; But it is nevertheless a maxim well established by experience, and generally acknowledged, where there has been sufficient experience, that the *aggregate* prosperity of manufactures, and the *aggregate* prosperity of Agriculture are intimately connected. In the Course of the discussion which has had place, various weighty considerations have been adduced operating in support of that maxim. Perhaps the superior steadiness of the demand of a domestic market for the surplus produce of the soil, is alone a convincing argument of its truth.

Ideas of a contrariety of interests between the Northern and southern regions of the Union, are in the Main as unfounded as they are mischievous. The diversity of Circumstances on which such contrariety is usually predicated, authorizes a directly contrary conclusion. Mutual wants constitute one of the strongest links of political connection, and the extent of these bears a natural proportion to the diversity in the means of mutual supply.

Suggestions of an opposite complexion are ever to be deplored, as unfriendly to the steady pursuit of one great common cause, and to the perfect harmony of all the parts.

In proportion as the mind is accustomed to trace the intimate connection of interest, which subsists between all the parts of a Society united under the *same* government—the infinite variety of channels which serve to Circulate the prosperity of each to and through the rest—in that proportion will it be little apt to be disturbed by solicitudes and Apprehensions which originate in local discriminations. It is a truth as important as it is agreeable, and one to which it is not easy to imagine exceptions, that everything tending to establish *substantial* and *permanent order*, in the affairs of a Country, to increase the total mass of industry and opulence, is ultimately beneficial to every part of it. On the Credit of this great truth, an acquiescence may safely be accorded, from every quarter, to all institutions and arrangements, which promise a confirmation of public order, and an augmentation of National Resource.

But there are more particular considerations which serve to fortify the idea, that the encouragement of manufactures is the interest of all parts of the Union. If the Northern and Middle states should be the principal scenes of such establishments, they would immediately benefit the More southern, by creating a demand for productions; some of which they have in common with the other states, and others of which are either peculiar to them, or more abundant, or of better quality, than elsewhere. These productions, principally are Timber, flax, Hemp, Cotton, Wool, raw silk, Indigo, iron, lead, furs, hides, skins and coals. Of these articles Cotton and Indigo are peculiar to the southern states; as are hitherto *Lead* and *Coal.* Flax and Hemp are or may be raised in greater abundance there, than in the More Northern states; and the Wool of Virginia is said to be of better quality than that of any other state: a Circumstance rendered the more probable by the reflection that Virginia embraces the same latitudes with the finest Wool Countries of Europe. The Climate of the south is also better adapted to the production of silk.

The extensive cultivation of Cotton can perhaps hardly be expected, but from the previous establishment of domestic Manufactories of the Article; and the surest encouragement and vent, for the others, would result from similar establishments in respect to them.

If then, it satisfactorily appears, that it is the Interest of the United states, generally, to encourage manufactures, it merits particular attention, that there are circumstances, which Render the present a critical moment for entering with Zeal upon the important business. The effort cannot fail to be materially seconded by a considerable and increasing influx of money, in consequence of foreign speculations in the funds—and by the disorders, which exist in different parts of Europe.

The first circumstance not only facilitates the execution of manufacturing enterprises; but it indicates them as a necessary mean to turn the thing itself to advantage, and to prevent its being eventually an evil. If useful employment be not found for the Money of foreigners brought to the country to be invested in purchases of the public debt, it will quickly be re-exported to defray the expense of an extraordinary consumption of foreign luxuries; and distressing drains of our specie may hereafter be experienced to pay the interest and redeem the principal of the purchased debt.

This useful employment too ought to be of a Nature to produce solid and permanent improvements. If the money merely serves to give a temporary spring to foreign commerce; as it cannot procure new and lasting outlets for the products of the Country; there will be no real or durable advantage gained. As far as it shall find its way in Agricultural ameliorations, in opening canals, and in similar improvements, it will be productive of substantial utility. But there is reason to doubt, whether in such channels it is likely to find sufficient employment, and still more whether many of those who possess it, would be as readily attracted to objects of this nature, as to manufacturing pursuits; which bear greater analogy to those to which they are accustomed, and to the spirit generated by them.

To open the one field, as well as the other, will at least secure a better prospect of useful employment, for whatever accession of money, there has been or may be.

There is at the present juncture a certain fermentation of mind, a certain activity of speculation and enterprise which if properly directed may be made subservient to useful purposes; but which if left entirely to itself, may be attended with pernicious effects.

The disturbed state of Europe, inclining its citizens to emigration, the requisite workmen will be more easily acquired than at another time; and the effect of multiplying the opportunities of employment to those who emigrate, may be an increase of the number and extent of valuable acquisitions to the population, arts, and industry of the Country.

To find pleasure in the calamities of other nations, would be criminal; but to benefit ourselves, by opening an asylum to those who suffer, in consequence of them, is as justifiable as it is politic.

A full view having now been taken of the inducements to the promotion of Manufactures in the United states, accompanied with an examination of the principal objections which are commonly urged in opposition, it is proper in the next place, to consider the means, by which it may be effected, as introductory to a Specification of the objects which in the present state of things appear the most fit to be encouraged, and of the particular measures which it may be advisable to adopt, in respect to each.

In order to a better judgment of the Means proper to be resorted to by the United states, it will be of use to Advert to those which have been employed with success in other Countries. The principal of these are:

I. Protecting duties—or duties on those foreign articles which are the rivals of the domestic ones, intended to be encouraged.

Duties of this Nature evidently amount to a virtual bounty on the domestic fabrics since by enhancing the charges on foreign Articles, they enable the National Manufacturers to undersell all their foreign Competitors. The propriety of this species of encouragement need not be dwelt upon; as it is not only a clear result from the numerous topics which have been suggested, but is sanctioned by the laws of the United States in a variety of instances; it has the additional recommendation of being a resource of revenue. Indeed all the duties imposed on imported articles, though with an exclusive view to Revenue, have the effect in Contemplation, and except where they fall on raw materials wear a beneficent aspect towards the manufactures of the Country.

II. Prohibitions of rival articles or duties equivalent to prohibitions.

This is another and an efficacious mean of encouraging national manufactures, but in general it is only fit to be employed when a manufacture, has made such a progress and is in so many hands as to ensure a due competition, and an adequate supply on reasonable terms. Of duties equivalent to prohibitions, there are examples in the Laws of the United States, and there are other Cases to which the principle may be advantageously extended, but they are not numerous.

Considering a monopoly of the domestic market to its own manufacturers as the reigning policy of manufacturing Nations, a similar policy on the part of the United States in every proper instance, is dictated, it might almost be said, by the principles of distributive justice; certainly by the duty of endeavoring to secure to their own Citizens a reciprocity of advantages.

III. Prohibitions of the exportation of the materials of manufactures.

The desire of securing a cheap and plentiful supply for the national workmen, and, where the article is either peculiar to the Country, or of peculiar quality there, the jealousy of enabling foreign workmen to rival those of the nation, with its own Materials, are the leading motives to this species of regulation. It ought not to be affirmed, that it is no instance proper, but it is certainly one which ought to be adopted with great circumspection and only in very plain Cases. It is seen at once, that its immediate operation, is to abridge the demand and keep down the price of the produce of some other branch of industry, generally speaking, of Agriculture, to the prejudice of those who carry it on; and though if it be really essential to the prosperity of any very important national Manufacture, it may happen that those who are injured in the first instance, may be eventually indemnified, by the superior steadiness of an extensive domestic market, depending on that prosperity: yet in a matter, in which there is so much room for nice and difficult combinations, in which such opposite considerations combat each other, prudence seems to dictate, that the expedient in question, ought to be indulged with a sparing hand.

IV. Pecuniary bounties.

This has been found one of the most efficacious means of encouraging manufactures, and it is in some views, the best. Though it has not yet been practiced upon by the Government of the United States (unless the allowances on the exportation of dried and pickled Fish and salted meat could be considered as a bounty) and though it is less favored by public opinion than some other modes. Its advantages, are these—

1. It is a species of encouragement more positive and direct than any other, and for that very reason, has a more immediate tendency to stimulate and uphold new enterprises, increasing the chances of profit, and diminishing the risks of loss, in the first attempts.

2. It avoids the inconvenience of a temporary augmentation of price, which is incident to some other modes, or it produces it to a less degree; either by making no addition to the charges on the rival foreign article, as in the Case of protecting duties, or by making a smaller addition. The first happens when the fund for the bounty is derived from a different object (which may or may not increase the price of some other article, according to

the nature of that object) the second, when the fund is derived from the same or a similar object of foreign manufacture. One percent duty on the foreign article converted into a bounty on the domestic, will have an equal effect with a duty of two percent, exclusive of such bounty; and the price of the foreign commodity is liable to be raised, in the one Case, in the proportion of 1 percent; in the other, in that of two percent. Indeed the bounty when drawn from another source is calculated to promote a reduction of price, because without laying any new charge on the foreign article, it serves to introduce a competition with it, and to increase the total quantity of the article in the Market.

3. Bounties have not like high protecting duties, a tendency to produce scarcity. An increase of price is not always the immediate, though, where the progress of a domestic Manufacture does not counteract a rise, it is commonly the ultimate effect of an additional duty. In the interval, between the laying of the duty and a proportional increase of price, it may discourage importation, by interfering with the profits to be expected from the sale of the article.

4. Bounties are sometimes not only the best, but the only proper expedient, for uniting the encouragement of a new object of agriculture, with that of a new object of manufacture. It is the Interest of the farmer to have the production of the raw material promoted, by counteracting the interference of the foreign material of the same kind. It is the interest of the manufacturer to have the material abundant and cheap. If prior to the domestic production of the Material, in sufficient quantity, to supply the manufacturer on good terms; a duty be laid upon the importation of it from abroad, with a view to promote the raising of it at home, the Interests both of the Farmer and Manufacturer will be disserved. By either destroying the requisite supply, or raising the price of the article, beyond what can be afforded to be given for it, by the Conductor of an infant manufacture, it is abandoned or fails; and there being no domestic manufactories to create a demand for the raw material, which is raised by the farmer, it is

in vain, that the Competition of the like foreign article may have been destroyed.

It cannot escape notice, that a duty upon the importation of an article can no otherwise aid the domestic production of it, than giving the latter greater advantages in the home market. It can have no influence upon the advantageous sale of the article produced, in foreign markets; no tendency, therefore to promote its exportation.

The true way to conciliate these two interests, is to lay a duty on foreign *manufactures* of the material, the growth of which is desired to be encouraged, and to apply the produce of that duty by way of bounty, either upon the production of the material itself or upon its manufacture at home or upon both. In this disposition of the thing, the Manufacturer commences his enterprise under every advantage, which is attainable, as to quantity or price, of the raw material: And the Farmer if the bounty be immediately to him, is enabled by it to enter into a successful competition with the foreign material; if the bounty be to the manufacturer on so much of the domestic material as he consumes, the operation is nearly the same; he has a motive of interest to prefer the domestic Commodity, if of equal quality, even at a higher price than the foreign, so long as the difference of price is anything short of the bounty which is allowed upon the article.

Except the stable and ordinary kinds of household Manufactures, or those for which there are very commanding local advantages, pecuniary bounties are in most cases indispensable to the introduction of a new branch. A stimulus and a support not less powerful and direct is generally speaking essential to the overcoming of the obstacles which arise from the Competitions of superior skill and maturity elsewhere. Bounties are especially essential, in regard to articles, upon which those foreigners, who have been accustomed to supply a Country, are in the practice of granting them.

The continuance of bounties on manufactures long established must almost always be of questionable policy: Because a presumption would arise in every such Case, that there were natural and inherent impediments to success. But in new undertakings, they are as justifiable, as they are oftentimes necessary.

There is a degree of prejudice against bounties from an appearance of giving away the public money, without an immediate consideration, and from a supposition, that they serve to enrich particular classes, at the expense of the Community.

But neither of these sources of dislike will bear a serious examination. There is no purpose, to which public money can be more beneficially applied, than to the acquisition of a new and useful branch of industry; no Consideration more valuable than a permanent addition to the general stock of productive labor.

As to the second source of objection, it equally lies against other modes of encouragement, which are admitted to be eligible. As often as a duty upon a foreign article makes an addition to its price, it causes an extra expense to the Community, for the benefit of the domestic manufacturer. A bounty does no more: But it is the Interest of the society in each case, to submit to a temporary expense, which is more than compensated, by an increase of industry and Wealth, by an augmentation of resources and independence; and by the circumstance of eventual cheapness, which has been noticed in another place.

It would deserve attention, however, in the employment of this species of encouragement in the United states, as a reason for moderating the degree of it in the instances, in which it might be deemed eligible, that the great distance of this country from Europe imposes very heavy charges on all the fabrics which are brought from thence, amounting from 15 to 30 Percent on their value, according to their bulk.

A Question has been made concerning the Constitutional right of the Government of the United States to apply this species of encouragement, but there is certainly no good foundation for such a question. The National Legislature has express authority "To lay and Collect taxes, duties, imposts and excises, to pay the debts and provide for the *Common defense* and *general welfare*" with no other qualifications than that "all duties, imposts and excises, shall be uniform throughout the United States, that no capitation or other direct tax shall be laid unless in proportion to numbers ascertained by a census or enumeration taken on the principles prescribed in the Constitution," and that "no tax or duty shall be laid on articles exported from any state." These three qualifications excepted, the power to *raise money* is *plenary*, and *indefinite*; and the objects to which it may be *appropriated* are no less comprehensive, than the payment of the public debts and the providing for the common defense and "*general Welfare.*" The terms "*general Welfare*" were doubtless intended to signify more than was expressed or imported in those which Preceded; otherwise numerous exigencies incident to the affairs of a Nation would have been left without a provision. The phrase is as comprehensive as any that could have been used; because it was not fit that the constitutional authority of the Union, to appropriate its revenues should have been restricted within narrower limits than the "General Welfare" and because this necessarily embraces a vast variety of particulars, which are susceptible neither of specification nor of definition.

It is therefore of necessity left to the discretion of the National Legislature, to pronounce, upon the objects, which concern the general Welfare, and for which under that description, an appropriation of money is requisite and proper. And there seems to be no room for a doubt that whatever concerns the general Interests of *learning of Agriculture*, of *Manufactures*, and of *Commerce* are within the sphere of the national Councils *as far as regards an application of Money*.

The only qualification of the generality of the Phrase in question, which seems to be admissible, is this—That the object to which an appropriation of money is to be made be *General* and not *local*; its operation extending in fact, or by possibility, throughout the Union, and not being confined to a particular spot.

No objection ought to arise to this construction from a supposition that it would imply a power to do whatever else should appear to Congress conducive to the General Welfare. A power to appropriate money with this latitude which is granted too in *express terms* would not carry a power to do any other thing, not authorized in the constitution, either expressly or by fair implication.

V. Premiums.

These are of a Nature allied to bounties, though distinguishable from them, in some important features.

Bounties are applicable to the whole quantity of an article produced, or manufactured, or exported, and involve a correspondent expense. Premiums serve to reward some particular excellence or superiority, some extraordinary exertion or skill, and are dispensed only in a small number of cases. But their effect is to stimulate general effort. Contrived so as to be both honorary and lucrative, they address themselves to different passions; touching the chords as well of emulation as of Interest. They are accordingly a very economical mean of exciting the enterprise of a Whole Community.

There are various Societies in different countries, whose object is the dispensation of Premiums for the encouragement of *Agriculture, Arts, manufactures,* and *Commerce*; and though they are for the most part voluntary associations, with comparatively slender funds, their utility has been immense. Much has been done by this mean in great Britain: Scotland in particular owes materially to it a prodigious amelioration of Condition. From a similar establishment in the United states, supplied and supported by the Government of the Union, vast benefits might reasonably be expected. Some further ideas on this head, shall accordingly be submitted, in the conclusion of this report.

VI. The Exemption of the Materials of manufactures from duty.

The policy of that Exemption as a general rule, particularly in reference to new Establishments, is obvious. It can hardly ever be advisable to add the obstructions of fiscal burdens to the difficulties which naturally embarrass a new manufacture; and where it is matured and in condition to become an object of revenue, it is generally speaking better that the fabric, than the Material should be the subject of Taxation. Ideas of proportion between the quantum of the tax and the value of the article, can be more easily adjusted, in the former, than in the latter case. An argument for exemptions of this kind in the United States, is to be derived from the practice, as far as their necessities have permitted, of those nations whom we are to meet as competitors in our own and in foreign Markets.

There are however exceptions to it; of which some examples will be given under the next head.

The Laws of the Union afford instances of the observance of the policy here recommended, but it will probably be found advisable to extend it to some other Cases. Of a nature, bearing some affinity to that policy is the regulation which exempts from duty the tools and implements, as well as the books, cloths and household furniture of foreign artists, who come to reside in the United states; an advantage already secured to them by the Laws of the Union, and which, it is in every view, proper to Continue.

VII. Drawbacks of the duties which are imposed on the Materials of Manufactures.

It has already been observed as a general rule that duties on those materials, ought with certain exceptions to be forborne. Of these exceptions, three cases occur, which may serve as examples—one, where the material is itself, an object of general or extensive consumption, and a fit and productive source of revenue: Another, where a manufacture or a simpler kind the competition of which with a like domestic article is desired to be restrained, partakes of the Nature of a raw material, from being capable, by a further process to be converted into a manufacture of a different kind, the introduction or growth of which is desired to be encouraged; a third where the Material itself is a production of the Country, and in sufficient abundance to furnish cheap and plentiful supply to the national Manufacturer.

Under the first description comes the article of Molasses. It is not only a fair object of revenue; but being a sweet, it is just that the consumers of it should pay a duty as well as the Consumers of sugar.

Cottons and linens in their White state fall under the second description. A duty upon such as are imported is proper to promote the domestic Manufacture of similar articles in the same state. A Drawback of that duty is proper to encourage the printing and staining at home of those which are brought from abroad: When the first of these manufactures has attained sufficient maturity in a Country, to furnish a full supply for the second, the utility of the drawback ceases.

The article of Hemp either now does or may be expected soon to exemplify the third Case, in the United states.

Where duties on the materials of manufactures are not laid for the purpose of preventing a competition with some domestic production, the same reasons which recommend, as a general rule, the exemption of those materials from duties, would recommend as a like General rule, the allowance of draw backs, in favor of the manufacturer. Accordingly such drawbacks are familiar in countries which systematically pursue the business of manufactures; which furnishes an argument for the observance of a similar policy in the United states; and the Idea has been adopted by the laws of the Union in the instances of salt and Molasses. It is believed that it will be found advantageous to extend it to some other Articles.

VIII. The encouragement of new inventions and discoveries, at home, and of the introduction into the United States of such as may have been made in other countries; particularly those, which relate to machinery.

This is among the most useful and unexceptionable of the aids, which can be given to manufactures. The usual means of that encouragement are pecuniary rewards, and, for a time, exclusive privileges. The first must be employed, according to the occasion, and the utility of the invention, or discovery: For the last, so far as respects "authors and inventors" provision has been made by Law. But it is desirable in regard to improvements and secrets of extraordinary value, to be able to extend the same benefit to Introducers, as well as Authors and Inventors; a policy which has been practiced with advantage in other countries. Here, however, as in some other cases, there is cause to regret, that the competency of the authority of the National Government to the good, which might be done, is not without a question. Many aids might be given to industry; many internal improvements of primary magnitude might be promoted, by an authority operating throughout the Union, which cannot be effected, as well, if at all, by an authority confined within the limits of a single state.

But if the legislature of the Union cannot do all the good, that might be wished, it is at least desirable, that all may be done, which is practicable. Means for promoting the introduction of foreign improvements, though less efficaciously than might be accomplished with more adequate authority, will form a part of the plan intended to be submitted in the close of this report.

It is customary with manufacturing nations to prohibit, under severe penalties, the exportation of implements and machines, which they have either invented or improved. There are already objects for a similar regulation in the United States; and others may be expected to occur from time to time. The adoption of it seems to be dictated by the principle of reciprocity. Greater liberality, in such respects, might better comport with the general spirit of the country; but a selfish and exclusive policy in other quarters will not always permit the free indulgence of a spirit, which would place us upon an unequal footing. As far as prohibitions tend to prevent foreign competitors from deriving the benefit of the improvements made at home, they tend to increase the advantages of those by whom they may have been introduced; and operate as an encouragement to exertion.

IX. Judicious regulations for the inspection of manufactured commodities.

This is not among the least important of the means, by which the prosperity of manufactures may be promoted. It is indeed in many cases one of the most essential. Contributing to prevent frauds upon consumers at home and exporters to foreign countries—to improve the quality and preserve the character of the national manufactures, it cannot fail to aid the expeditious and advantageous Sale of them, and to serve as a guard against successful competition from other quarters. The reputation of the flour and lumber of some states, and of the Pot ash of others has been established by an attention to this point. And the like good name might be procured for those articles, wheresoever produced, by a judicious and uniform system of Inspection; throughout the ports of the United States. A like system might also be extended with advantage to other commodities.

X. The facilitating of pecuniary remittances from place to place—

Is a point of considerable moment to trade in general, and to manufactures in particular; by rendering more easy the purchase of raw materials and provisions and the payment for manufactured supplies. A general circulation of Bank paper, which is to be expected from the institution lately established will be a most valuable mean to this end. But much good would also accrue from some additional provisions respecting inland bills of exchange. If those drawn in one state payable in another were made negotiable, everywhere, and interest and damages allowed in case of protest, it would greatly promote negotiations between the Citizens of different states, by rendering them more secure; and, with it the convenience and advantage of the Merchants and manufacturers of each.

XI. The facilitating of the transportation of commodities.

Improvements favoring this object intimately concern all the domestic interests of a community; but they may without impropriety be mentioned as having an important relation to manufactures. There is perhaps scarcely any thing, which has been better calculated to assist the manufactures of Great Britain, than the ameliorations of the public roads of that Kingdom, and the great progress which has been of late made in opening canals. Of the former, the United States stand much in need; and for the latter they present uncommon facilities.

The symptoms of attention to the improvement of inland Navigation, which have lately appeared in some quarters, must fill with pleasure every breast warmed with a true Zeal for the prosperity of the Country. These examples, it is to be hoped, will stimulate the exertions of the Government and the Citizens of every state. There can certainly be no object, more worthy of the cares of the local administrations; and it were to be wished, that there was no doubt of the power of the national Government to lend its direct aid, on a comprehensive plan. This is one of those improvements, which could be prosecuted with more efficacy by the whole, than by any part or parts of the Union. There are cases in which the general interest will be in danger to be sacrificed to the collision of some supposed local interests. Jealousies, in matters of this kind, are as apt to exist, as they are apt to be erroneous.

The following remarks are sufficiently judicious and pertinent to deserve a literal quotation. "Good roads, canals, and navigable rivers, by diminishing the expense of carriage, put the *remote parts of a country* more nearly upon a level with those in the neighborhood of the town. They are *upon that account* the greatest of all improvements. They encourage the cultivation of the remote, which must always be the most extensive circle of the country. They are advantageous to the Town by breaking down the monopoly of the country in its neighborhood. They are advantageous *even to that part of the Country.* Though they introduce some rival commodities into the old Market, they open many new markets to its produce. Monopoly besides is a great enemy to good management, which can never be universally established, but in consequence of that free and universal competition, which forces everybody to have recourse to it for the sake of self-defense. It is not more than Fifty years ago that *some of the counties in the neighborhood of London petitioned the Parliament, against the extension of the turnpike roads, into the remoter counties.*

Those remoter counties, they pretended, from the cheapness of Labor, would be able to sell their grass and corn cheaper in the London Market, than themselves, and they would thereby reduce their rents and ruin their cultivation. Their rents however have risen and their cultivation has been improved, since that time."

Specimens of a spirit, similar to that which governed the counties here spoken of present themselves too frequently to the eye of an impartial observer, and render it a wish of patriotism, that the body in this Country, in whose councils a local or partial spirit is least likely to predominate, were at liberty to pursue and promote the general interest, in those instances, in which there might be danger of the interference of such a spirit.

The foregoing are the principal of the means, by which the growth of manufactures is ordinarily promoted. It is, however, not merely necessary, that the measures of government, which have a direct view to manufactures, should be calculated to assist and protect them, but that those which only collaterally affect them, in the general course of the administration, should be guarded from any peculiar tendency to injure them.

There are certain species of taxes, which are apt to be oppressive to different parts of the community, and among other ill effects have a very unfriendly aspect towards manufactures. All Poll or Capitation taxes are of this nature. They either proceed, according to a fixed rate, which operates unequally, and injuriously to the industrious poor; or they vest a discretion in certain officers, to make estimates and assessments which are necessarily vague, conjectural and liable to abuse. They ought therefore to be abstained from, in all but cases of distressing emergency.

All such taxes (including all taxes on occupations) which proceed according to the amount of capital *supposed* to be employed in a business, or of profits *supposed* to be made in it are unavoidably hurtful to industry. It is in vain, that the evil may be endeavored to be mitigated by leaving it, in the first instance, in the option of the party to be taxed, to declare the amount of his capital or profits.

Men engaged in any trade of business have commonly weighty reasons to avoid disclosures, which would expose, with anything like accuracy, the real state of their affairs. They most frequently find it better to risk oppression, than to avail themselves of so inconvenient a refuge. And the consequence is, that they often suffer oppression.

When the disclosure too, if made, is not definitive, but controllable by the discretion, or in other words, by the passions and prejudices of the revenue officers, it is not only an ineffectual protection, but the possibility of its being so is an additional reason for not resorting to it.

Allowing to the public officers the most equitable dispositions; yet where they are to exercise a discretion, without certain data, they cannot fail to be often misled by appearances. The quantity of business, which seems to be going on, is, in a vast number of cases, a very deceitful criterion of the profits which are made; yet it is perhaps the best they can have, and it is the one, on which they will most naturally rely. A business therefore which may rather require aid, from the government, than be in a capacity to be contributory to it, may find itself crushed by the mistaken conjectures of the Assessors of taxes.

Arbitrary taxes, under which denomination are comprised all those, that leave the *quantum* of the tax to be raised on each person, to the *discretion* of certain officers, are as contrary to the genius of liberty as to the maxims of industry. In this light, they have been viewed by the most judicious observers on government; who have bestowed upon them the severest epithets of reprobation; as constituting one of the worst features usually to be met with in the practice of despotic governments.

It is certain at least, that such taxes are particularly inimical to the success of manufacturing industry, and ought carefully to be avoided by a government, which desires to promote it.

The great copiousness of the subject of this Report has insensibly led to a more lengthy preliminary discussion, than was originally contemplated, or intended. It appeared proper to investigate principles, to consider objections, and to endeavor to establish the utility of the thing proposed to be encouraged; previous to a specification of the objects which might occur, as meriting or requiring encouragement, and of the measures, which might be proper, in respect to each. The first purpose having been fulfilled, it remains to pursue the second. In the selection of objects, five circumstances seem entitled to particular attention; the capacity of the Country to furnish the raw material—the degree in which the nature of the manufacture admits of a substitute for manual labor in machinery—the facility of execution—the extensiveness of the uses, to which the article can be applied—its subserviency to other interests, particularly the great one of national defense. There are however objects, to which these circumstances are little applicable, which for some special reasons, may have a claim to encouragement.

A designation of the principal raw material of which each manufacture is composed will serve to introduce the remarks upon it. As, in the first place—

Iron

The manufactures of this article are entitled to preeminent rank. None are more essential in their kinds, nor so extensive in their uses. They constitute in whole or in part the implements or the materials or both of almost every useful occupation. Their instrumentality is everywhere conspicuous.

It is fortunate for the United States that they have peculiar advantages for deriving the full benefit of this most valuable material, and they have every motive to improve it, with systematic care. It is to be found in various parts of the United States, in great abundance and of almost every quality; and fuel, the chief instrument in manufacturing it, is both cheap and plenty. This particularly applies to Charcoal; but there are productive coal mines already in operation, and strong indications, that the material is to be found in abundance, in a variety of other places.

The inquiries to which the subject of this report has led have been answered with proofs that manufactories of Iron, though generally understood to be extensive, are far more so than is commonly supposed. The kinds, in which the greatest progress has been made, have been mentioned in another place, and need not be repeated; but there is little doubt that every other kind, with due cultivation, will rapidly succeed. It is worthy of remark that several of the particular trades, of which it is the basis, are capable of being carried on without the aid of large capitals.

Iron works have very greatly increased in the United States and are prosecuted, with much more advantage than formerly. The average price before the revolution was about Sixty four Dollars Per Ton—at present it is about Eighty; a rise which is chiefly to be attributed to the increase of manufactures of the material.

The still further extension and multiplication of such manufactures will have the double effect of promoting the extraction of the Metal itself, and of converting it to a greater number of profitable purposes.

Those manufactures too unite in a greater degree, than almost any others, the several requisities, which have been mentioned, as proper to be consulted in the selection of objects.

The only further encouragement of manufactories of this article, the propriety of which may be considered as unquestionable, seems to be an increase of the duties on foreign rival commodities.

Steel is a branch which has already made a considerable progress, and it is ascertained that some new enterprises, on a more extensive scale, have been lately set on foot. The facility of carrying it to all extent which will supply all internal demands, and furnish a considerable surplus for exportation, cannot be doubted. The duty upon the importation of this article, which is, at present, seventy-five cents per cwt. may, it is conceived, be safely and advantageously extended to one hundred cents. It is desirable, by decisive arrangements, to second the efforts which are making in so very valuable a branch.

The United States already, in a great measure, supply themselves with nails and spikes. They are able, and ought certainly to do it, entirely. The first and most laborious operation, in this manufacture, is performed by water-mills; and of the persons afterwards employed, a great proportion are boys, whose early habits of industry are of importance to the community, to the present support of their families, and to their own future comfort. It is not less curious than true, that, in certain parts of the country, the making of nails is an occasional family manufacture.

The expediency of an additional duty on these articles, is indicated by an important fact. About 1,800,000 pounds of them were imported into the United States, in the course of a year, ending the 30th of September, 1790. A duty of two cents per pound would, it is presumable, speedily put an end to so considerable an importation. And it is, in every view, proper that an end should be put to it.

The manufacture of these articles, like that of some others, suffers from the carelessness and dishonesty of a part of those who carry it on. An inspection in certain cases might tend to correct the evil. It will deserve consideration whether a regulation of this sort cannot be applied, without inconvenience, to the exportation of the articles, either to foreign countries, or from one state to another.

The implements of husbandry are made in several states in great abundance. In many places, it is done by the common blacksmiths. And there is no doubt that an ample supply for the whole country can, with great ease, be procured among ourselves.

Various kinds of edged tools for the use of mechanics are also made; and a considerable quantity of hollow wares, though the business of castings has not yet attained the perfection which might be wished. It is, however, improving, and as there are respectable capitals, in good hands, embarked in the prosecution of those branches of iron manufactories, which are yet in their infancy, they may all be contemplated as objects not difficult to be acquired.

To insure the end, it seems equally safe and prudent, to extend the duty, ad valorem, upon all manufactures of iron, or of which iron is the article of chief value, to ten percent.

Fire-arms and other military weapons may, it is conceived, be placed, without inconvenience, in the class of articles rated at fifteen percent. There are, already, manufactories of these articles, which only require the stimulus of a certain demand to render them adequate to the supply of the United States.

It would, also, be a material aid to manufactures of this nature, as well as a mean of public security, if provision should be made for an annual purchase of military weapons, of home manufacture, to a certain determinate extent, in order to the formation of arsenals; and to replace, from time to time, such as should be drawn for use, so as always to have in store the quantity of each kind which should be deemed a competent supply.

But it may, hereafter, deserve legislative consideration, whether manufactories of all the necessary weapons of war ought not to be established, on account of the government itself. Such establishments are agreeable to the usual practice of nations, and that practice seems founded on sufficient reason.

There appears to be an improvidence in leaving these essential instruments of national defense to the casual speculations of individual adventure; a resource which can less be relied upon, in this case, than in most others; the articles in question not being objects of ordinary and indispensable private consumption or use. As a general rule, manufactories on the immediate account of government are to be avoided; but this seems to be one of the few exceptions which that rule admits, depending on very special reasons.

Manufactures of steel, generally, or of which steel is the article of chief value, may, with advantage, be placed in the class of goods rated at seven and a half percent. As manufactures of this kind have not yet made any considerable progress, it is a reason for not rating them as high as those of iron; but, as this material is the basis of them, and as their extension is not less practicable than important, it is desirable to promote it by a somewhat higher duty than the present.

A question arises, how far it might be expedient to permit the importation of iron, in pigs and bars, free from duty. It would certainly be favorable to manufactures of the article; but the doubt is, whether it might not interfere with its production.

Two circumstances, however, abate, if they do not remove apprehension, on this score; one is, the considerable increase of price which has been already remarked, and which renders it probable that the free admission of foreign iron would not be inconsistent with an adequate profit to the proprietors of iron-works; the other is the augmentation of demand which would be likely to attend the increase of manufactures of the article in consequence of the additional encouragements proposed to be given. But caution nevertheless, in a matter of this kind, is most advisable. The measure suggested ought, perhaps, rather to be contemplated subject to the lights of further experience, than immediately adopted.

Copper

The manufactures of which this article is susceptible are also of great extent and utility. Under this description, those of brass, of which it is the principal ingredient, are intended to be included.

The material is a natural production of the country. Mines of copper have actually been wrought, and with profit to the undertakers, though it is not known that any are now in this condition. And no thing is easier than the introduction of it from other countries on moderate terms, and in great plenty.

Coppersmiths and brass-founders, particularly the former, are numerous in the United States; some of whom carry on business to a respectable extent.

To multiply and extend manufactories of the materials in question, is worthy of attention and effort. In order to this, it is desirable to facilitate a plentiful supply of the materials. And a proper mean to this end is, to place them in the class of free articles. Copper in plates and brass are already in this predicament; but copper in pigs and bars is not; neither is *lapis calaminaris*, which, together with *copper* and *charcoal*, constitute the component ingredients of brass. The exemption from duty, by parity of reason, ought to embrace all such of these articles as are objects of importation.

An additional duty on brass wares, will tend to the general end in view. These now stand at five percent, while those of tin, pewter, and copper, are rated at seven and an half. There appears to be a propriety, in every view, in placing brass wares upon the same level with them; and it merits consideration, whether the duty upon all of them, ought not to be raised to ten percent.

Lead

There are numerous proofs, that this material abounds in the United States, and requires little to unfold it to an extent more than equal to every domestic occasion. A prolific mine of it has long been open in the south-western parts of Virginia, and under a public administration, during the late war, yielded a considerable supply for military use. This is now in the hands of individuals, who not only carry it on with spirit, but have established manufactories of it at Richmond, in the same state.

The duties already laid upon the importation of this article, either in its unmanufactured or manufactured state, insure it a decisive advantage in the home market—which amounts to considerable encouragement. If the duty on pewter wares should be raised, it would afford a further encouragement. Nothing else occurs as proper to be added.

Fossil Coal

This, as an important instrument of manufactures, may, without impropriety, be mentioned among the subjects of this report.

A copious supply of it would be of great consequence to the

iron branch. As an article of household fuel, also, it is an interesting production; the utility of which must increase in proportion to the decrease of wood, by the progress of settlement and cultivation. And its importance to navigation, as an immense article of transportation coast-wise, is signally exemplified in Great-Britain.

It is known, that there are several coal mines in Virginia, now worked; and appearances of their existence are familiar in a number of places.

The expediency of a bounty on all this species of coal of home production, and of premiums on the opening of new mines, under certain qualifications, appears to be worthy of particular examination. The great importance of the article will amply justify a reasonable expense in this way, if it shall appear to be necessary to, and shall be thought likely to answer, the end.

Wood

Several manufactures of this article flourish in the United States. Ships are nowhere built in greater perfection, and cabinet-wares, generally, are made little, if at all, inferior to those of Europe. Their extent is such as to have admitted of considerable exportation.

An exemption from duty of the several kinds of wood ordinarily used in these manufactures, seems to be all that is requisite by way of encouragement. It is recommended, by the consideration of a similar policy being pursued in other countries, and by the expediency of giving equal advantages to our own workmen in wood. The abundance of timber proper for ship-building in the United States, does not appear to be any objection to it. The increasing scarcity, and growing importance of that article in the European countries, admonish the United States to commence, and systematically to pursue, measures for the preservation of their stock. Whatever may promote the regular establishment of magazines of ship timber, is, in various views, desirable.

Skins

There are scarcely any manufactories of greater importance, than of this article. Their direct and very happy influence upon agriculture, by promoting the raising of cattle of different kinds, is a very material recommendation.

It is pleasing, too, to observe the extensive progress they have made in their principal branches; which are so far matured as almost to defy foreign competition. Tanneries, in particular, are not only carried on as a regular business, in numerous instances, and in various parts of the country, but they constitute, in some places, a valuable item of incidental family manufactures.

Representations, however, have been made, importing the expediency of further encouragement to the leather branch, in two ways; one, by increasing the duty on the manufactures of it, which are imported; the other, by prohibiting the exportation of bark. In support of the latter it is alleged, that the price of bark, chiefly in consequence of large exportations, has risen, within a few years, from about three dollars, to four and an half per cord.

These suggestions are submitted rather as intimations which merit considerations, than as matters, the propriety of which is manifest. It is not clear, that an increase of duty is necessary; and in regard to the prohibition desired, there is no evidence of any considerable exportation hitherto; and it is most probable, that whatever augmentation of price may have taken place, is to be attributed to an extension of the home demand from the increase of manufactures, and to a decrease of the supply, in consequence of the progress of settlement, rather than to the quantities which have been exported.

It is mentioned, however, as an additional reason for the prohibition, that one species of the bark usually exported, is in some sort peculiar to the country; and the material of a very valuable dye, of great use in some other manufactures in which the United States have begun a competition.

There may also be this argument in favor of an increase of duty. The object is of importance enough to claim decisive encouragement; and the progress which has been made, leaves no room to apprehend any inconvenience on the score of supply from such an increase.

It would be of benefit to this branch, if glue, which is now rated at five percent, were made the object of an excluding duty. It is already made in large quantities at various tanneries; and, like paper, is an entire economy of materials, which, if not manufactured, would be left to perish. It may be placed with advantage in the class of articles paying fifteen percent.

Grain

Manufactures of the several species of this article, have a title to peculiar favor; not only because they are most of them immediately connected with the subsistence of the citizens, but because they enlarge the demand for the most precious products of the soil. Though flour may with propriety be noticed as a manufacture of grain, it were useless to do it, but for the purpose of submitting the expediency of a general system of inspection throughout the ports of the United States; which, if established upon proper principles, would be likely to improve the quality of our flour everywhere, and to raise its reputation in foreign markets. There, are, however, considerations which stand in the way of such an arrangement.

Ardent spirits and malt liquors are, next to flour, the two principal manufactures of grain. The first has made a very extensive, the last a considerable progress in the United States. In respect to both, an exclusive possession of the home market ought to be secured to the domestic manufacturers, as fast as circumstances will admit. Nothing is more practicable, and nothing more desirable.

The existing laws of the United States have done much towards attaining this valuable object; but some additions to the present duties on foreign distilled spirits, and foreign malt liquors, and, perhaps, an abatement of those on home-made spirits, would more effectually secure it; and there does not occur any very weighty objection to either.

An augmentation of the duties on imported spirits, would favor, as well the distillation of spirits from molasses, as that from grain. And to secure to the nation the benefit of a manufacture, even of foreign materials, is always of great, though perhaps of secondary importance.

A strong impression prevails in the minds of those concerned in distilleries, (including, too, the most candid and enlightened,) that greater differences in the rates of duty on foreign and domestic spirits, are necessary completely to secure the successful manufacture of the latter; and there are facts which entitle this impression to attention.

It is known, that the price of molasses, for some years past, has been successively rising in the West-India markets, owing partly to a competition which did not formerly exist, and partly to an extension of demand in this country; and it is evident, that the late disturbances in those Islands, from which we draw our principal supply, must so far interfere with the production of the article, as to occasion a material enhancement of price. The destruction and devastation attendant on the insurrection in Hispaniola in particular, must not only contribute very much to that effect, but may be expected to give it some duration. These circumstances, and the duty of three cents per gallon on molasses, may render it difficult for the distillers of that material to maintain, with adequate profit, a competition with the rum brought from the West-Indies, the quality of which is so considerably superior.

The consumption of Geneva, or gin, in this country, is extensive. It is not long since distilleries of it have grown up among us, to any importance. They are now becoming of consequence, but being still in their infancy, they require protection.

It is represented, that the price of some of the materials is greater here than in Holland, from which place large quantities are brought—the price of labor considerably greater—the capitals engaged in the business there, much larger than those which are employed here—the rate of profits, at which the undertakers can afford to carry it on, much less—the prejudices in favor of imported gin, strong.

These circumstances are alleged, to outweigh the charges which attend the bringing of the article from Europe to the United States, and the present difference of duty, so as to obstruct the prosecution of the manufacture with due advantage.

Experiment could, perhaps, alone decide with certainty the justness of the suggestions which are made; but in relation to branches of manufacture so important, it would seem inexpedient to hazard an unfavorable issue, and better to err on the side of too great, than of too small, a difference in the particular in question.

It is, therefore, submitted, that an addition of two cents per gallon be made to the duty on imported spirits of the first class of proof, with a proportionable increase on those of higher proof; and that a deduction of one cent per gallon be made from the duty on spirits distilled within the United States, beginning with the first class of proof, and a proportionable deduction from the duty on those of higher proof.

It is ascertained, that by far the greatest part of the malt liquors consumed in the United States, are the produce of domestic breweries. It is desirable, and, in all likelihood, attainable, that the whole consumption should be supplied by ourselves.

The malt liquors made at home, though inferior to the best, are equal to a great part of those which have been usually imported. The progress already made, is an earnest of what may be accomplished. The growing competition is an assurance of improvement. This will be accelerated by measures tending to invite a greater capital into this channel of employment.

To render the encouragement of domestic breweries decisive, it may be advisable to substitute to the present rates of duty, eight cents per gallon generally; and it will deserve to be considered as a guard against invasions, whether there ought not to be a prohibition of their importation, except in casks of considerable capacity. It is to be hoped, that such a duty would banish from the market foreign malt liquors of inferior quality; and that the best kind only would continue to be imported, till it should be supplanted by the efforts of equal skill or care at home.

Till that period, the importation so qualified, would be a useful stimulus to improvement; and in the mean time, the payment of the increased price for the enjoyment of a luxury, in order to the encouragement of a most useful branch of domestic industry, could not reasonably be deemed a hardship.

As a further aid to manufactures of grain, though upon a smaller scale, the articles of starch, hair-powder, and wafers, may with great propriety be placed among those which are rated at fifteen percent. No manufactures are more simple, nor more completely within the reach of a full supply from domestic sources; and it is a policy, as common as it is obvious, to make them the objects either of prohibitory duties, or of express prohibition.

Flax and Hemp

Manufactures of these articles have so much affinity to each other, and they are so often blended, that they may with advantage be considered in conjunction. The importance of the linen branch to agriculture—its precious effects upon household industry—the ease with which the materials can be produced at home to any requisite extent—the great advances which have been already made in the coarser fabrics of them, especially in the family way, constitute claims of peculiar force to the patronage of government.

This patronage may be afforded in various ways by promoting the growth of the materials; by increasing the impediments to an advantageous competition of rival foreign articles; by direct bounties or premiums upon the home manufacture.

First. *As to promoting the growth of the materials.*

In respect to hemp, something has been already done by the high duty upon foreign hemp. If the facilities for domestic production were not unusually great, the policy of the duty on the foreign raw material, would be highly questionable, as interfering with the growth of manufactures of it. But making the proper allowances for those facilities, and with an eye to the future and natural progress of the country, the measure does not appear, upon the whole, exceptionable.

A strong wish naturally suggests itself, that some method could be devised, of affording a more direct encouragement to the growth both of flax and hemp; such as would be effectual, and at the same time not attended with too great inconveniences. To this end, bounties and premiums offer themselves to consideration; but no modification of them has yet occurred, which would not either hazard too much expense, or operate unequally in reference to the circumstances of different parts of the Union; and which would not be attended with very great difficulties in the execution.

Secondly. *As to increasing the impediments to an advantageous competition of rival foreign articles.*

To this purpose, an augmentation of the duties on importation is the obvious expedient; which, in regard to certain articles, appears to be recommended by sufficient reasons.

The principal of these articles is sail-cloth; one intimately connected with navigation and defense; and of which a flourishing manufactory is established at Boston, and very promising ones at several other places.

It is presumed to be both safe and advisable to place this in the class of articles rated at 10 percent. A strong reason for it results from the consideration that a bounty of two pence sterling per ell is allowed in Great-Britain, upon the exportation of the sail-cloth manufactured in that kingdom.

It would likewise appear to be good policy to raise the duty to seven and an half percent on the following articles: Drillings, Osnaburghs, Ticklenburghs, Dowlas, Canvas, Brown Rolls, Bagging, and upon all other linens, the first cost of which at the place of exportation does not exceed 35 cents per yard. A bounty of 12 ½ percent upon an average, on the exportation of such or similar linens from Great-Britain, encourages the manufacture of them in that country, and increases the obstacles to a successful competition in the countries to which they are sent.

The quantities of tow and other household linens manufactured in different parts of the United States, and the expectations which are derived from some late experiments, of being able to extend the use of labor-saving machines in the coarser fabrics of linen, obviate the danger of inconvenience from an increase of the duty upon such articles, and authorize a hope of speedy and complete success to the endeavors which may be used for procuring an internal supply.

Thirdly. *As to direct bounties or premiums upon the manufactured articles.*

To afford more effectual encouragement to the manufacture, and at the same time to promote the cheapness of the article for the benefit of navigation, it will be of great use to allow a bounty of two cents per yard on all sail-cloth which is made in the United States from materials of their own growth. This would also assist the culture of those materials. An encouragement of this kind, if adopted, ought to be established for a moderate term of years, to invite to new undertakings, and to an extension of the old. This is an article of importance enough to warrant the employment of extraordinary means in its favor.

Cotton

There is something in the texture of this material which adapts it in a peculiar degree to the application of machines. The signal utility of the mill for spinning of cotton, not long since invented in England, has been noticed in another place; but there are other machines scarcely inferior in utility, which, in the different manufactories of this article, are employed either exclusively, or with more than ordinary effect. This very important circumstance recommends the fabrics of cotton, in a more particular manner, to a country in which a defect of hands constitutes the greatest obstacle to success.

The variety and extent of the uses to which the manufactures of this article are applicable, is another powerful argument in their favor.

And the faculty of the United States to produce the raw material in abundance, and of a quality which, though alleged to be inferior to some that is produced in other quarters, is, nevertheless, capable of being used with advantage in many fabrics, and is probably susceptible of being carried, by a more experienced culture, to much greater perfection, suggests an additional and a very cogent inducement to the vigorous pursuit of the cotton branch, in its several subdivisions.

How much has been already done, has been stated in a preceding part of this report.

In addition to this, it may be announced, that a society is forming with a capital which is expected to be extended to at least half a million of dollars; on behalf of which, measures are already in train for prosecuting, on a large scale, the making and printing of cotton goods.

These circumstances conspire to indicate the expediency of removing any obstructions which may happen to exist to the advantageous prosecution of the manufactories in question, and of adding such encouragements as may appear necessary and proper.

The present duty of three cents per pound on the foreign raw material, is undoubtedly a very serious impediment to the progress of those manufactories.

The injurious tendency of similar duties, either prior to the establishment, or in the infancy of the domestic manufacture of the article, as it regards the manufacture; and their worse than inutility, in relation to the home production of the material itself, have been anticipated, particularly in discussing the subject of pecuniary bounties.

Cotton has not the same pretensions with hemp to form an exception to the general rule.

Not being, like hemp, an universal production of the country, it affords less assurance of an adequate internal supply; but the chief objection arises from the doubts which are entertained concerning the quality of the national cotton. It is alleged, that the fiber of it is considerably shorter and weaker than that of some other places; and it has been observed as a general rule, that the nearer the place of growth to the equator, the better the quality of the cotton. That which comes from Cayenne, Suriname, and Demerara, is said to be preferable, even at a material difference of price, to the cotton of the islands.

While a hope may reasonably be indulged, that with due care and attention, the national cotton may be made to approach nearer than it now does to that of regions somewhat more favored by climate; and while facts authorize an opinion, that very great use may be made of it, and that it is a resource which gives greater security to the cotton fabrics of this country, than can be enjoyed by any which depends wholly on external supply, it will certainly be wise in every view, to let our infant manufactures have the full benefit of the best materials on the cheapest terms. It is obvious that the necessity of having such materials, is proportioned to the unskillfulness and inexperience of the workmen employed, who, if inexpert, will not fail to commit great waste, where the materials they are to work with are of an indifferent kind.

To secure to the national manufacturers so essential an advantage, a repeal of the present duty on imported cotton is indispensable.

A substitute for this, far more encouraging to domestic production, will be to grant a bounty on the national cotton, when wrought at a home manufactory; to which a bounty on the exportation of it may be added. Either, or both, would do much more towards promoting the growth of the article, than the merely nominal encouragement, which it is proposed to abolish. The first would also have a direct influence in encouraging the manufacture.

The bounty which has been mentioned as existing in Great-Britain upon the exportation of coarse linens not exceeding a certain value, applies also to certain descriptions of cotton goods of similar value.

This furnishes an additional argument for allowing to the national manufacturers the species of encouragement just suggested, and indeed for adding some other aid.

One cent per yard, not less than of a given width, on all goods of cotton, or of cotton and linen mixed, which are manufactured in the United States, with the addition of one cent per pound weight of the material, if made of national cotton, would amount to an aid of considerable importance, both to the production and to the manufacture of that valuable article. And it is conceived, that the expense would be well justified by the magnitude of the object.

The printing and staining of cotton goods, is known to be a distinct business from the fabrication of them. It is one easily accomplished, and which, as it adds materially to the value of the article in its white state, and prepares it for a variety of new uses, is of importance to be promoted.

As imported cottons, equally with those which are made at home, may be the objects of this manufacture, it will merit consideration, whether the whole, or a part of the duty, on the white goods, ought not to be allowed to be drawn back in favor of those who print or stain them. This measure would certainly operate as a powerful encouragement to the business; and though it may in a degree counteract the original fabrication of the articles, it would probably more than compensate for this disadvantage in the rapid growth of a collateral branch which is of a nature sooner to attain to maturity. When a sufficient progress shall have been made, the drawback may be abrogated, and by that time the domestic supply of the articles to be printed or stained, will have been extended.

If the duty of seven and an half percent on certain kinds of cotton goods were extended to all goods of cotton, or of which it is the principal material, it would probably more than counterbalance the effect of the drawback proposed in relation to the fabrication of the article. And no material objection occurs to such an extension. The duty, then, considering all the circumstances which attend goods of this description, could not be deemed inconveniently high; and it may be inferred from various causes that the prices of them would still continue moderate.

Manufactories of cotton goods not long since established at Beverly in Massachusetts, and at Providence, in the state of Rhode-Island, and conducted with a perseverance corresponding with the patriotic motives which began them, seem to have overcome the first obstacles to success; producing corduroys, velvets, fustians, jeans, and other similar articles, of a quality which will bear a comparison with the like articles brought from Manchester. The one at Providence has the merit of being the first in introducing into the United States the celebrated cotton mill; which not only furnishes materials for that manufactory itself, but for the supply of private families for household manufacture.

Other manufactories of the same material, as regular businesses, have also been begun at different places in the state of Connecticut, but all upon a smaller scale than those above mentioned. Some essays are also making in the printing and staining of cotton goods. There are several small establishments of this kind already on foot.

Wool

In a country, the climate of which partakes of so considerable a proportion of winter as that of a great part of the United States, the woolen branch cannot be regarded as inferior to any which relates to the clothing of the inhabitants.

Household manufactures of this material are carried on in different parts of the United States to a very interesting extent; but there is only one branch which, as a regular business, can be said to have acquired maturity. This is the making of hats.

Hats of wool, and of wool mixed with fur, are made in large quantities in different states; and nothing seems wanting but an adequate supply of materials to render the manufacture commensurate with the demand.

A promising essay towards the fabrication of cloths, cashmeres, and other woolen goods, is likewise going on at *Hartford*, in Connecticut. Specimens of the different kinds which are made, in the possession of the Secretary, evince that these fabrics have attained a very considerable degree of perfection. Their quality certainly surpasses anything that could have been looked for in so short a time, and under so great disadvantages; and conspires with the scantiness of the means, which have been at the command of the directors, to form the eulogium of that public spirit, perseverance, and judgment, which have been able to accomplish so much.

To cherish and bring to maturity this precious embryo, must engage the most ardent wishes, and proportionable regret, as far as the means of doing it may appear difficult or uncertain.

Measures which should tend to promote an abundant supply of wool of good quality, would probably afford the most efficacious aid that present circumstances permit.

To encourage the raising and improving the breed of sheep at home, would certainly be the most desirable expedient for that purpose; but it may not be alone sufficient, especially as it is yet a problem, whether our wool be capable of such a degree of improvement, as to render it fit for the finer fabrics.

Premiums would probably be found the best means of promoting the domestic, and bounties the foreign supply. The first may be within the compass of the institution hereafter to be submitted; the last would require a specific legislative provision. If any bounties are granted, they ought, of course, to be adjusted with an eye to quality as well as quantity.

A fund for this purpose may be derived from the addition of two and an half percent to the present rate of duty on carpets and carpeting; an increase, to which the nature of the articles suggests no objection, and which may at the same time furnish a motive the more to the fabrication of them at home; towards which some beginnings have been made.

Silk

The production of this article is attended with great facility in most parts of the United States. Some pleasing essays are making in Connecticut, as well towards that, as towards the manufacture of what is produced. Stockings, Handkerchiefs, Ribbons, and Buttons, are made, though as yet but in small quantities.

A manufactory of Lace, upon a scale not very extensive, has been long memorable at Ipswich, in the State of Massachusetts.

An exemption of the material from the duty which it now pays on importation, and premiums upon the production, to be dispensed under the direction of the Institution before alluded to, seem to be the only species of encouragement advisable at so early a stage of the thing.

Glass

The materials for making glass are found everywhere. In the United States there is no deficiency of them. The sands and stones called Tarso, which include flinty and crystalline substances generally, and the salts of various plants, particularly of the sea-weed kali, or kelp, constitute the essential ingredients. An extraordinary abundance of fuel, is a particular advantage enjoyed by this country for such manufactures. They, however, require large capitals, and involve much manual labor.

Different manufactories of glass are now on foot in the United States. The present duty of twelve and an half percent on all imported articles of glass, amount to a considerable encouragement to those manufactories. If anything in addition is judged eligible, the most proper would appear to be a direct bounty on window-glass and black bottles.

The first recommends itself as an object of general convenience; the last adds to that character, the circumstance of being an important item in breweries. A complaint is made of great deficiency in this respect.

Gun-Powder

No small progress has been of late made in the manufacture

of this very important article. It may, indeed, be considered as already established; but its high importance renders its further extension very desirable.

The encouragements which it already enjoys, are a duty of ten percent on the foreign rival article, and an exemption of saltpeter, one of the principal ingredients of which it is composed, from duty. A like exemption of sulphur, another chief ingredient, would appear to be equally proper. No quantity of this article has yet been produced from internal sources. The use made of it in finishing the bottoms of ships, is an additional inducement to placing it in the class of free goods. Regulations for the careful inspection of the article would have a favorable tendency.

Paper

Manufactories of paper are among those which are arrived at the greatest maturity in the United States, and are most adequate to national supply. That of paper-hangings is a branch in which respectable progress has been made.

Nothing material seems wanting to the further success of this valuable branch, which is already protected by a competent duty on similar imported articles.

In the enumeration of the several kinds made subject to that duty, sheathing and cartridge paper have been omitted. These being the most simple manufactures of the sort, and necessary to military supply, as well as ship-building, recommend themselves, equally with those of other descriptions, to encouragement, and appear to be as fully within the compass of domestic exertions.

Printed Books

The great number of presses disseminated throughout the Union, seem to afford an assurance, that there is no need of being indebted to foreign countries for the printing of the books which are used in the United States. A duty of ten percent instead of five, which is now charged upon the article, would have a tendency to aid the business internally.

It occurs, as an objection to this, that it may have an unfavorable aspect towards literature, by raising the prices of books in universal use in private families, schools, and other seminaries of learning. But the difference it is conceived would be without effect.

As to books which usually fill the libraries of the wealthier classes, and of professional men, such an augmentation of prices, as might be occasioned by an additional duty of five percent would be too little felt to be an impediment to the acquisition.

And with regard to books which may be specially imported for the use of particular seminaries of learning, and of public libraries, a total exemption from duty would be advisable, which would go towards obviating the objection just mentioned. They are now subject to a duty of five percent.

As to the books in most general family use, the constancy and universality of the demand, would ensure exertions to furnish them at home, and the means are completely adequate. It may also be expected ultimately, in this as in other cases, that the extension of the domestic manufacture would conduce to the cheapness of the article.

It ought not to pass unremarked, that to encourage the printing of books, is to encourage the manufacture of paper.

Refined Sugars and Chocolate
Are among the number of extensive and prosperous domestic manufactures.

Drawbacks of the duties upon the materials of which they are respectively made, in cases of exportation, would have a beneficial influence upon the manufacture, and would conform to a precedent, which has been already furnished in the instance of molasses, on the exportation of distilled spirits.

Cocoa—the raw material now pays a duty of one cent per pound, while chocolate, which is a prevailing and very simple manufacture, is comprised in the mass of articles rated at no more than five percent.

There would appear to be a propriety in encouraging the manufacture, by a somewhat higher duty on its foreign rival, than is paid on the raw material. Two cents per pound on imported chocolate, would, it is presumed, be without inconvenience.

The foregoing heads comprise the most important of the several kinds of manufactures, which have occurred as requiring, and, at the same time, as most proper for public encouragement; and such measures for affording it, as have appeared best calculated to answer the end, have been suggested.

The observations, which have accompanied this delineation of objects, supersede the necessity of many supplementary remarks. One or two however may not be altogether superfluous.

Bounties are in various instances proposed as one species of encouragement.

It is a familiar objection to them that they are difficult to be managed and liable to frauds. But neither that difficulty nor this danger seems sufficiently great to countervail the advantages of which they are productive, when rightly applied. And it is presumed to have been shown, that they are in some cases, particularly in the infancy of new enterprises indispensable.

It will however be necessary to guard, with extraordinary circumspection, the manner of dispensing them. The requisite precautions have been thought of; but to enter into the detail would swell this report, already voluminous, to a size too inconvenient.

If the principle shall not be deemed inadmissible the means of avoiding an abuse of it will not be likely to present insurmountable obstacles. There are useful guides from practice in other quarters.

It shall therefore only be remarked here, in relation to this point, that any bounty, which may be applied to the manufacture of an article, cannot with safety extend beyond those manufactories, at which the making of the article is a regular trade.

It would be impossible to annex adequate precautions to a benefit of that nature, if extended to every private family, in which the manufacture was incidentally carried on, and its being a merely incidental occupation which engages a portion of time that would otherwise be lost, it can be advantageously carried on, without so special an aid.

The possibility of a diminution of the revenue may also present itself, as an objection to the arrangements, which have been submitted.

But there is no truth, which may be more firmly relied upon, than that the interests of the revenue are promoted, by whatever promotes an increase of National industry and wealth.

In proportion to the degree of these, is the capacity of every country to contribute to the public treasury; and where the capacity to pay is increased, or even is not decreased, the only consequence of measures, which diminish any particular resource is a change of the object. If by encouraging the manufacture of an article at home, the revenue, which has been wont to accrue from its importation, should be lessened, an indemnification can easily be found, either out of the manufacture itself, or from some other object, which may be deemed more convenient.

The measures however, which have been submitted, taken aggregately, will for a long time to come rather augment than decrease the public revenue.

There is little room to hope, that the progress of manufactures, will so equally keep pace with the progress of population, as to prevent, even, a gradual augmentation of the product of the duties on imported articles.

As, nevertheless, an abolition in some instances, and a reduction in others of duties, which have been pledged for the public debt, is proposed, it is essential, that it should be accompanied with a competent substitute. In order to this, it is requisite, that all the additional duties which shall be laid, be appropriated in the first instance, to replace all defalcations, which may proceed from any such abolition or diminution. It is evident, at first glance, that they will not only be adequate to this, but will yield a considerable surplus.

This surplus will serve:

First. To constitute a fund for paying the bounties which shall have been decreed.

Secondly. To constitute a fund for the operations of a Board, to be established, for promoting Arts, Agriculture, Manufactures and Commerce. Of this institution, different intimations have been given, in the course of this report. An outline of a plan for it shall now be submitted.

Let a certain annual sum, be set apart, and placed under the management of Commissioners, not less than three, to consist of certain Officers of the Government and their Successors in Office.

Let these Commissioners be empowered to apply the fund confided to them—to defray the expenses of the emigration of Artists, and Manufacturers in particular branches of extraordinary importance—to induce the prosecution and introduction of useful discoveries, inventions and improvements, by proportionate rewards, judiciously held out and applied—to encourage by premiums both honorable and lucrative the exertions of individuals, and of classes, in relation to the several objects, they are charged with promoting and to afford such other aids to those objects, as may be generally designated by law.

The Commissioners to render to the Legislature an annual account of their transactions and disbursements; and all such sums as shall not have been applied to the purposes of their trust, at the end of every three years, to revert to the Treasury. It may also be enjoined upon them, not to draw out the money, but for the purpose of some specific disbursement.

It may moreover be of use, to authorize them to receive voluntary contributions; making it their duty to apply them to the particular objects for which they may have been made, if any shall have been designated by the donors.

There is reason to believe, that the progress of particular manufactures has been much retarded by the want of skillful workmen. And it often happens that the capitals employed are not equal to the purposes of bringing from abroad workmen of a superior kind. Here, in cases worthy of it, the auxiliary agency of Government would in all probability be useful. There are also valuable workmen, in every branch, who are prevented from emigrating solely by the want of means. Occasional aids to such persons properly administered might be a source of valuable acquisitions to the country.

The propriety of stimulating by rewards, the invention and introduction of useful improvements, is admitted without difficulty. But the success of attempts in this way must evidently depend much on the manner of conducting them. It is probable, that the placing of the dispensation of those rewards under some proper discretionary direction, where they may be accompanied by collateral expedients, will serve to give them the surest efficacy. It seems impracticable to apportion, by general rules, specific compensations for discoveries of unknown and disproportionate utility.

The great use which may be made of a fund of this nature to procure and import foreign improvements is particularly obvious. Among these, the article of machines would form a most important item.

The operation and utility of premiums have been adverted to; together with the advantages which have resulted from their dispensation, under the direction of certain public and private societies. Of this some experience has been had in the instance of the Pennsylvania Society for the Promotion of Manufactures and useful Arts; but the funds of that association have been too contracted to produce more than a very small portion of the good to which the principles of it would have led. It may confidently be affirmed that there is scarcely any thing, which has been devised, better calculated to excite a general spirit of improvement than the institutions of this nature. They are truly invaluable.

In countries where there is great private wealth, much may be effected by the voluntary contributions of patriotic individuals, but in a community situated like that of the United States, the public purse must supply the deficiency of private resource. In what can it be so useful as in prompting and improving the efforts of industry?

All which is humbly submitted
    Alexander Hamilton
    Secretary of the Treasury

The Four New Laws to Save The U.S.A. Now! Not an Option: An Immediate Necessity

Lyndon H. LaRouche, Jr.
June 10, 2014

The Fact of the Matter

The economy of the United States of America, and also that of the trans-Atlantic political-economic regions of the planet, are now under the immediate, mortal danger of a general, physical-economic, chain-reaction breakdown-crisis of that region of this planet as a whole. The name for that direct breakdown-crisis throughout those indicated regions of the planet, is the presently ongoing introduction of a general "Bail-in" action under several or more governments of that region: the effect on those regions, will be comparable to the physical-economic collapse of the post-"World War I" general collapse of the economy of the German Weimar Republic: but, this time, hitting, first, the entirety of the nation-state economies of the trans-Atlantic region, rather than some defeated economies within Europe. A chain-reaction collapse, to this effect, is already accelerating with an effect on the money-systems of the nations of that region. The present acceleration of a "Bail-in" policy throughout the trans-Atlantic region, as underway now, means mass-death suddenly hitting the populations of all nations within that trans-Atlantic region: whether directly, or by "overflow."

The effects of this already prepared action by the monetarist interests of that so-designated region, unless stopped virtually now, will produce, in effect, an accelerating rate of genocide throughout that indicated portion of the planet immediately, but, also, with catastrophic "side effects" of comparable significance in the Eurasian regions.

The Available Remedies

The only location for the immediately necessary action which could prevent such an immediate genocide throughout the trans-Atlantic sector of the planet, requires the U.S. Government's now immediate decision *to institute four specific, cardinal measures: measures which must be fully consistent with the specific intent of the original U.S. Federal Constitution, as had been specified by U.S. Treasury Secretary Alexander Hamilton while he remained in office: (1) immediate re-enactment of the Glass-Steagall law instituted by U.S. President Franklin D. Roosevelt, without modification, as to principle of action. (2) A return to a system of top-down, and thoroughly defined, National Banking.*

The actually tested, successful model to be authorized is that which had been instituted, under the direction of the policies of national banking which had been actually, successfully installed under President Abraham Lincoln's superseding authority of a currency created by the Presidency of the United States (e.g. "Greenbacks"), as conducted as *a national banking-and-credit-system placed under the supervision of the Office of the Treasury Secretary of the United States.*

For the present circumstances, all other banking and currency policies, are to be superseded, or, simply, discontinued, as follows. Banks qualifying for operations under this provision, shall be assessed for their proven competence to operate as under the national authority for creating and composing the elements of this essential practice, which had been assigned, as by tradition, to the original office of Secretary of the U.S. Treasury under Alexander Hamilton. This means that the individual states of the United States are under national standards of practice, and, not any among the separate states of our nation.

(3) The purpose of the use of a Federal Credit-system, is to generate high-productivity trends in improvements of employment, with the accompanying intention, to increase the physical-economic productivity, and the standard of living of the persons and households of the United States. The creation of credit for the now urgently needed increase of the relative quality and quantity of productive employment, must be assured, this time, once more, as was done successfully under President Franklin D. Roosevelt, or by like standards of Federal practice used to create a general economic recovery of the nation, per capita, and for rate of net effects in productivity, and by reliance on the essential human principle, which distinguishes the human personality from the systemic characteristics of the lower forms of life: the net rate of increase of the energy-flux density of effective practice. This means intrinsically, a thoroughly scientific, rather than a merely mathematical one, and by the related increase of the effective energy-flux density per capita, and for the human population when considered as a whole. The ceaseless increase of the physical-productivity of employment, accompanied by its benefits for the general welfare, are a principle of Federal law which must be a paramount standard of achievement of the nation and the individual.

(4) "Adopt a Fusion-Driver 'Crash Program.'" The essential distinction of man from all lower forms of life, hence, in practice, is that it presents the means for the perfection of the specifically affirmative aims and needs of human individual and social life. Therefore: the subject of man in the process of creation, as an affirmative identification of an affirmative statement of an absolute state of nature, is a permitted form of expression. Principles of nature are either only affirmation, or they could not be affirmatively stated among civilized human minds.

Given the circumstances of the United States, in particular, since the assassinations of President John F. Kennedy, and his brother, Robert, the rapid increase required for even any recovery of the U.S. economy, since that time, requires nothing less than measures taken and executed by President Franklin D. Roosevelt during his actual term in office. The victims of the evil brought upon the United States and its population since the strange death of President Harding, under Presidents Calvin Coolidge and Herbert Hoover (like the terrible effects of the Bush-Cheney and Barack Obama administrations, presently) require remedies comparable to those of President Franklin Roosevelt while he were in office.

This means emergency relief measures, including sensible temporary recovery measures, required to stem the tide of death left by the Coolidge-Hoover regimes: measures required to preserve the dignity of what were otherwise the unemployed, while building up the most powerful economic and warfare capabilities assembled under the President Franklin Roosevelt Presidency for as long as he remained alive in office. This meant the mustering of the power of nuclear power, then, and means thermonuclear fusion now. Without that intent and its accomplishment, the population of the United States in particular, faces, now, immediately, the most monstrous disaster in its history to date. In principle, without a Presidency suited to remove and dump the worst effects felt presently, those created presently by the Bush-Cheney and Obama Presidencies, the United States were soon finished, beginning with the mass-death of the U.S. population under the Obama Administration's recent and now accelerated policies of practice.

There are certain policies which are most notably required, on that account, now, as follows:

Vernadsky on Man & Creation

V.I. Vernadsky's systemic principle of human nature, is a universal principle, which is uniquely specific to the crucial factor of the existence of the human species. For example: "time" and "space" do not actually exist as a set of metrical principles of the Solar system; their admissible employment for purposes of communication is essentially a nominal presumption. Since competent science for today can be expressed only in terms of the unique characteristic of the human species' role within the known aspects of the universe, the human principle is the only true principle known to us for practice: the notions of space and time are merely useful imageries.

Rather:

The essential characteristic of the human species, is its distinction from all other species of living processes: that, as a matter of principle, which is rooted scientifically, for all competent modern science, on the foundations of the principles set forth by Filippo Brunelleschi (the discoverer of the ontological minimum), Nicholas of Cusa (the discovery of the ontological maximum), and the positive discovery by mankind, by Johannes Kepler, of a principle coincident with the perfected Classical human singing scale adopted by Kepler, and the elementary measure of the Solar System within the still larger universe of the Galaxy, and higher orders in the universe.

Or, similarly, later, the modern physical-scientific standard implicit in the argument of Bernhard Riemann, the actual minimum (echoing the principle of Brunelleschi), of Max Planck, the actual maximum of the present maximum, that of Albert Einstein; and, the relatively latest, consequent implications of the definition of human life by Vladimir Ivanovich Vernadsky. These values are, each relative absolutes of measurement of man's role within the knowledge of the universe.

This set of facts pertains to the inherent fraud of the merely mathematicians and the modernist "musical performers" since the standard of the relevant paragon for music, Johannes Brahms (prior to the degenerates, such as the merely mathematicians, such as David Hilbert and the true model for every modern Satan, such as Bertrand Russell, or Tony Blair).

The knowable measure, in principle, of the difference between man and all among the lower forms of life, is found in what has been usefully regarded as the naturally upward evolution of the human species, in contrast to all other known categories of living species. The standard of measurement of these compared relationships, is that mankind is enabled to evolve upward, and that categorically, by those voluntarily noëtic powers of the human individual will.

Except when mankind appears in a morally and physically degenerate state of behavior, such as within the cultures of the tyrants Zeus, the Roman Empire, and the British empire, presently: all actually sane cultures of mankind, have appeared, this far, in a certain fact of evolutionary progress from the quality of an inferior, to a superior species. This, when considered in terms of efficient effects, corresponds, within the domain of a living human practice of chemistry, to a form of systemic advances, even now leaps, in the chemical energy-flux density of society's increase of the effective energy-flux-density of scientific and comparable expressions of leaps in progress of the species itself: in short, a universal physical principle of human progress.

The healthy human culture, such as that of Christianity, if they warrant this affirmation of such a devotion, for example, represents a society which is increasing the powers of its productive abilities for progress, to an ever higher level of per-capita existence. The contrary cases, the so-called "zero-growth" scourges, such as the current British empire are, systemically, a true model consistent with the tyrannies of a Zeus, or, a Roman Empire, or a British (better said) "brutish" empire, such as the types, for us in the United States, of the Bush-Cheney and Obama administrations, whose characteristic has been, concordant with that of such frankly Satanic models as that of Rome and the British empire presently, a shrinking human population of the planet, a population being degraded presently in respect to its intellectual and physical productivity, as under those U.S. Presidencies, most recently.

Chemistry: The Yardstick of History

We call it "chemistry." Mankind's progress, as measured rather simply as a species, is expressed typically in the rising power of the principle of human life, over the abilities of animal life generally, and relatively absolute superiority over the powers of non-living processes to achieve within mankind's willful intervention to that intended effect. Progress exists so only under a continuing, progressive increase of the productive and related powers of the human species. That progress defines the absolute distinction of the human species from all others presently known to us. A government of people based on a policy of "zero-population growth and per capita standard of human life" is a moral, and practical abomination.

Man is mankind's only true measure of the history of our Solar system, and what reposes within it. That is the same thing, as the most honored meaning and endless achievement of the human species, now within nearby Solar space, heading upward to mastery over the Sun and its Solar system, the one discovered (uniquely, as a matter of fact), by Johannes Kepler.

A Fusion economy, is the presently urgent next step, and standard, for man's gains of power within the Solar system, and, later, beyond.

CPSIA information can be obtained
at www.ICGtesting.com
Printed in the USA
BVHW041315050720
582987BV00005B/280